Euripides And His Age

Gilbert Murray

EURIPIDES AND HIS AGE

BY

GILBERT MURRAY
LL.D., D.LITT., F.B.A.

REGIUS PROFESSOR OF GREEK IN THE UNIVERSITY
OF OXFORD

NEW YORK
HENRY HOLT AND COMPANY
LONDON
WILLIAMS AND NORGATE

THE UNIVERSITY PRESS, CAMBRIDGE, U.S.A.

CONTENTS

▼

CONTENTS

EURIPIDES AND HIS AGE

CHAPTER I

INTRODUCTORY

MOST of the volumes of this series are occupied with large subjects and subjects commonly recognized as important to great masses of people at the present day. In devoting the present volume to the study of a single writer, remote from us in time and civilization and scarcely known by more than name to many readers of the Library, I am moved by the belief that, quite apart from his disputed greatness as a poet and thinker, apart from his amazing and perhaps unparalleled success as a practical playwright, Euripides is a figure of high significance in the history of humanity and of special interest to our own generation.

Born, according to the legend, in exile and fated to die in exile, Euripides, in whatever light one regards him, is a man of curious and ironic history. As a poet he has lived through the ages in an atmosphere of con-

7

troversy, generally—though by no means
always—loved by poets and despised by
critics. As a thinker he is even to this day
treated almost as a personal enemy by
scholars of orthodox and conformist minds;
defended, idealized and sometimes transformed beyond recognition by various cham-
pions of rebellion and the free intellect. The
greatest difficulty that I feel in writing about
him is to keep in mind without loss of pro-
portion anything like the whole activity of
the many-sided man. Recent writers have
tended to emphasize chiefly his work as a
destructive thinker. Dr. Verrall, the most
brilliant of all modern critics of Euripides, to
whose pioneer work my own debt is greater
than I can well express, entitled one of his
books "Euripides the Rationalist" and followed to its extreme limit the path indicated
by this particular clue. His vivid and interesting disciple Professor Norwood has
followed him. In Germany Dr. Nestlé, in a
sober and learned book, treating of Euripides
as a thinker, says that "all mysticism was
fundamentally repugnant to him"; a view
which is certainly wrong, since some of the
finest expressions of Greek mysticism known
to us are taken from the works of Euripides.
Another good writer, Steiger, draws an elabo-

rate parallel between Euripides and Ibsen
and finds the one key to Euripides in his
realism and his absolute devotion to truth.
Yet an older generation of Euripides-lovers
felt these things quite differently. When
Macaulay proclaimed that there was absolutely nothing in literature to equal *The
Bacchae*, he was certainly not thinking about
rationalism or realism. He felt the romance,
the magic, the sheer poetry. So did Milton
and Shelley and Browning. And so did the
older English scholars like Porson and Elmsley. Porson, while admitting that the critics
have many things to say against Euripides
as compared, for instance, with Sophocles,
answers in his inarticulate way *"illum ad-
miramur, hunc legimus"*—"we admire the
one, but we read the other." Elmsley, so
far from regarding Euripides as mainly a
thinker, remarks in passing that he was a
poet singularly addicted to contradicting
himself. To Porson and Elmsley the poetry
of Euripides might or might not be good on
the highest plane, it was at any rate delight-
ful. Quite different again are the momentous judgments pronounced upon him as a
writer of tragedy by two of the greatest
judges. Aristotle, writing at a period when
Euripides was rather out of fashion, and

subjecting him to much serious and sometimes unintelligent criticism, considers him
still "the most tragic of the poets." And
Goethe, after expressing his surprise at the
general belittling of Euripides by "the aris-
tocracy of philologists, led by the buffoon
Aristophanes," asks emphatically: "Have
all the nations of the world since his time
produced one dramatist who was worthy to
hand him his slippers?" (Tagebüchern, No-
vember 22, 1831.) We must try, if we can,
to bear duly in mind all these different lines
of approach.

As a playwright the fate of Euripides has
been strange. All through a long life he
was almost invariably beaten in the State
competitions. He was steadily admired by
some few philosophers, like Socrates; he
enjoyed immense fame throughout Greece;
but the official judges of poetry were against
him, and his own people of Athens admired
him reluctantly and with a grudge.

After death, indeed, he seemed to come
into his kingdom. He held the stage as no
other tragedian has ever held it, and we hear
of his plays being performed with popular
success six hundred years after they were
written, and in countries far removed from

Greece. He influenced all the higher forms
of Greek writing, both in prose and poetry.
He is more quoted by subsequent writers
than any other Greek tragedian; nay, if we
leave out of count mere dictionary references
to rare words, he is more quoted than all the
other tragedians together. And nineteen of
his plays have survived to our own day as
against seven each of Aeschylus and Sophocles. This seems enough glory for any man.
Yet the fate that grudged him prizes in his
lifetime contrived afterwards to spread a
veneer of commonplaceness over the success
which it could not prevent. To a great extent Euripides was read because he was, or
seemed, easy; the older poets were neglected
because they were difficult. Attic Greek in
his hands had begun to assume the form in
which it remained for a thousand years as
the recognized literary language of the east
of Europe and the great instrument and
symbol of civilization. He was a treasure-
house of Attic style and ancient maxims,
and eminently useful to orators who liked
quotations. Meantime the melody and
meaning of his lyrics were lost, because men
had forgotten the pronunciation of fifth-
century Greek and could no longer read
lyrics intelligently. The obviously exciting

quality of his plays kept its effect; but there
was no one to understand the subtlety of his
craftsmanship, the intimate study of character, the skilful forging of links and clashes
between scenes, the mastery of that most
wonderful of Greek dramatic instruments,
the Chorus. Plays had practically ceased to
be written. They were thought of either as
rhetorical exercises or as spectacles for the
amphitheatre. Something similar happened
to the whole inward spirit in which he worked,
call it philosophy or call it religion.   Its
meaning became obscured. It had indeed
a powerful influence on the philosophers of
the great fourth century schools: they probably understood at least one side of him.
But the sayings of his that are quoted broad-
cast and repeated through author after author of the decadence are mostly thoughts of
quite the second rank, which have lost half
their value by being torn from their context,
often commonplace, often—as is natural in
fragments of dramas—mutually contradic-
tory, though almost always simply and
clearly expressed.

It was this clear expression which the late
Greeks valued so highly. "Clarity"—*sa-
phèneia*—was the watchword of style in
Euripides' own day and remained always the

foremost aim of Greek rhetoric. Indeed what a Greek called "rhetorikê" often implied the very opposite of what we call "rhetoric." To think clearly, to arrange your matter under formal heads, to have each paragraph definitely articulated and each sentence simply and exactly expressed: that was the main lesson of the Greek rhetor. The tendency was already beginning in classical times and no classical writer carried it further than Euripides. But here again Fate has been ironical with him. The ages that were incapable of understanding him loved him for his clearness: our own age, which might at last understand him, is instinctively repelled by it. We do not much like a poet to be very clear, and we hate him to be formal. We are clever readers, quick in the up-take, apt to feel flattered and stimulated by a little obscurity; mystical philosophy is all very well in a poet, but clear-cut intellect—no. At any rate we are sharply offended by "firstlys, secondlys and thirdlys," by divisions on the one hand and on the other hand. And all this and more Euripides insists on giving us.

It is the great obstacle between him and us. Apart from it we have only to exercise a little historical imagination and we shall find in him a man, not indeed modern—half his

charm is that he is so remote and austere—
but a man who has in his mind the same
problems as ourselves, the same doubts and
largely the same ideals; who has felt the same
desires and indignations as a great number
of people at the present day, especially young
people. Not because young people are
cleverer than old, nor yet because they are
less wise; but because the poet or philosopher or martyr who lives, half-articulate,
inside most human beings is apt to be
smothered or starved to death in the course
of middle life. As long as he is still alive
we have, most of us, the key to understanding Euripides.

What, then, shall be our method in approaching him? It is fatal to fly straight at
him with modern ready-made analogies. We
must see him in his own atmosphere. Every
man who possesses real vitality can be seen
as the resultant of two forces. He is first the
child of a particular age, society, convention;
of what we may call in one word a tradition.
He is secondly, in one degree or another, a
rebel against that tradition. And the best
traditions make the best rebels. Euripides
is the child of a strong and splendid tradition and is, together with Plato, the fiercest
of all rebels against it.

There is nothing paradoxical in this. No
tradition is perfect. The best brings only a
passing period of peace or triumph or stable
equilibrium; humanity rests for a moment,
but knows that it must travel further; to
rest for ever would be to die. The most
thorough conformists are probably at their
best when forced to fight for their ideal
against forces that would destroy it. And a
tradition itself is generally at its best, not
when it is universally accepted, but when it
is being attacked and broken. It is then
that it learns to search its own heart and live
up to its full meaning. And in a sense the
greatest triumph that any tradition can ac-
complish is to rear noble and worthy rebels.
The Greek tradition of the fifth century B.C.,
the great age of Athens, not only achieved
extraordinary advances in most departments
of human life, but it trained an extraordinary band of critical or rebellious children.
Many a reader of Plato's most splendid
satires against democratic Athens will feel
within him the conclusive answer: "No
place but Athens could ever have reared
such a man as this, and taught him to see
these faults or conceive these ideals."

We are in reaction now against another
great age, an age whose achievements in art

are memorable, in literature massive and
splendid, in science and invention absolutely
unparalleled, but greatest of all perhaps in
the raising of all standards of public duty,
the humanizing of law and society, and the
awakening of high ideals in social and inter-
national politics. The Victorian Age had,
amid enormous differences, a certain simi-
larity with the Periclean in its lack of self-
examination, its rush and chivalry and
optimism, its unconscious hypocrisy, its
failure to think out its problems to the bitter
end. And in most of the current criticism
on things Victorian, so far as it is not mere
fashion or folly, one seems to feel the Victorian spirit itself speaking. It arraigns
Victorian things by a Victorian standard;
blames them not because they have moved
in a particular direction, but because they
have not moved far enough; because so
many of the things they attempted are still
left undone, because the ideals they preached
and the standards by which they claimed to
be acting were so much harder of satisfaction
than they knew. Euripides, like ourselves,
comes in an age of criticism following upon
an age of movement and action. And for
the most part, like ourselves, he accepts the
general standards on which the movement

and action were based. He accepts the Athenian ideals of free thought, free speech, democracy, "virtue" and patriotism. He arraigns his country because she is false to them.

We have spoken of the tradition as a homogeneous thing, but for any poet or artist there are two quite different webs in it. There are the accepted conventions of his art and the accepted beliefs of his intellect, the one set aiming at the production of beauty, the others at the attainment of truth.

Now for every artist who is also a critic or rebel there is a difference of kind between these two sets of conventions. For the purposes of truth the tradition is absolutely indifferent. If, as a matter of fact, the earth goes round the sun, it does so not a whit the less because most ages have believed the opposite. The seeker for truth can, as far as truth is concerned, reject tradition without a qualm. But with art the case is different. Art has to give a message from one man to another. As you can only speak to a man in a language which you both know, so you can only appeal to his artistic side by means of some common tradition. His natural ex-

pectation, whether we try to satisfy or to
surprise it, to surpass or to disappoint it, is
always an essential element in the artistic
effect. Consequently the tradition cannot
be disregarded.

This distinction is often strongly marked
in the practice of different artists. One poet
may be both a pioneer of new roads in thought
and a breaker of the laws of technique, like
Walt Whitman—an enemy of the tradition
in both kinds. Another may be slack and
anarchical in his technique though quite
conventional in his thought. I refrain from
suggesting instances. Still more clearly there
are poets, such as Shelley or Swinburne,
whose works are full of intellectual rebellion
while their technique is exquisite and elaborate. The thoughts are bold and strange.
The form is the traditional form developed
and made more exquisite.

Now Euripides, except for some so-called
licences in metre, belongs in my judgment
markedly to the last class. In speculation
he is a critic and a free lance; in artistic form
he is intensely traditional. He seems to have
loved the very stiffnesses of the form in
which he worked. He developed its inherent
powers in ways undreamed of, but he never
broke the mould or strayed away into shape-

lessness or mere realism. His last, and in
many respects his greatest, play, the *Bacchae*,
is, as far as our evidence goes, the most
formal that he ever wrote.

These, then, are the lights in which we
propose to look at Euripides. In attempting
to reconstruct his life we must be conscious
of two backgrounds against which he will be
found standing, according as we regard him
as Thinker or as pure Artist. We must first
try to understand something of the tradition
of thought in which he was reared, that is the
general atmosphere of fifth century Athens,
and watch how he expressed it and how he
reacted against it. Next, we must understand what Greek tragedy was, what rituals
and conventions held it firm, and what inner
fire kept it living, and so study the method
in which Euripides used it for his chosen
mode of expression, obeying its laws and at
the same time liberating its spirit.

CHAPTER II

IT is in one sense impossible to write a life
of Euripides, for the simple reason that he
lived too long ago. In his time people were
only just beginning to write history at all;
Herodotus, the "father of history," was his
close contemporary. They had begun to
record really great events; but it had not
occurred to them that the life of any individual was worth all the trouble of tracing
out and writing down. Biography of a sort
began about two generations afterwards,
when the disciples of Aristotle and Epicurus
exerted themselves to find out and record
the lives of their masters. But biography
in our sense—the complete writing of a life
year by year with dates and documents—was
never practised at all in antiquity. Think of
the Gospels, of the Acts, even of Tacitus'
Life of Agricola. They are different one from

another, but they are all unlike any modern biography in their resolute indifference to anything like completeness. Ancient "Lives" as a rule select a few great deeds, a few great sayings or discourses; they concentrate upon the last years of their subject and often especially upon his death.

The dates at which various eminent men of antiquity died are well known. The man was then famous and his death was a memorable event. But—except in a few aristocratic states, like Cos, which records the actual birthday of the great physician Hippocrates —no baby was eminent and not many young men. Very few dates of birth are known; and in the case of almost all the famous men of antiquity their early histories are forgotten and their early works lost. So it is with Euripides.

History in later antiquity was chiefly a branch of *belles lettres* and made no great effort after exactness. As a rule it contented itself with the date at which a man "flourished," a very rough conception, conventionally fixed either by the time when he did his most memorable work or the year when he reached the age of forty. The year commonly assigned to Euripides' birth is a good instance of ancient method in these things.

The system of chronology was badly confused. In the first place there was no generally accepted era from which to date; and
even if there had been, the numerical system,
before the invention of Arabic ciphers, was
as confused as English spelling is at the
present day, and made it hard to do the
simplest sums. So the ordinary educational
plan was to group events together in some
scheme that might not be quite exact but
was calculated to have some symbolic interest and to stay in the memory. For instance, the three great tragedians were
grouped together round the Battle of Salamis, the great triumph of the Persian Wars
in 480 B.C. Aeschylus fought among the
heavy-armed infantry. Sophocles danced
in a choir of boys to celebrate the victory,
and Euripides was born in Salamis on the
day of the battle. We do not know the
origin of this pleasant fable; but we have
another date given in a very ancient chronicle
called the *Parian Marble*, which was found
in the island of Paros in the seventeenth
century and was composed in the year 264
B.C. It puts the birth of Euripides in 484
B.C., and since we cannot find any reason
why this year should be invented, and since
the *Marble* is the oldest witness now extant,

we shall probably do well provisionally to accept its statement.

In some of the MSS. which preserve Euripides' plays there are "scholia" or ancient traditional commentaries written round the margin. A few of the oldest notes in them come from Alexandrian scholars who lived in the second century B.C. Others date from Roman times, in the first few centuries of the Christian era; others from the eleventh century and even later. And among them there is a quite ancient document called *Life and Race of Euripides*.

It is anonymous and shapeless. Sentences may have been added or omitted by the various people who at different times have owned or copied the MSS. But we can see that it is derived from early sources, and notably from a "Life" which was written by one Satyrus, a writer of the Peripatetic or Aristotelian school, towards the end of the third century B.C. Fragments from the same source have been detected in the Latin authors Varro and Gellius; and it has influenced the biographical notice in the ancient Greek lexicon of Suidas (tenth century A.D.). Suidas used also another earlier and better source, the *Attic Chronicle* of Philochorus.

Philochorus was a careful and systematic

annalist of the early third century B.C., who
used official documents and verified his statements. His main work was to record all that
affected Athens—history, myths, festivals
and customs, but he also wrote various
special treatises, one of which was *On Euripides*. Satyrus wrote a series of *Lives of
Famous Men*, which was very popular, and
we are now—since 1911—in a position to
judge how undeserved its popularity was.
For fragments of his *Life of Euripides* have
been unearthed in Egypt by Drs. Grenfell
and Hunt and published in their *Oxyrrhyncus
Papyri*, vol. ix. The life takes the form of a
dialogue—apparently a dialogue with a lady.
It is a mass of quotations, anecdotes, bits of
literary criticism, all run together with an
air of culture and pleasantness, a spice of
gallantry and a surprising indifference to
historical fact. Evidently anecdotes amused
Satyrus and facts, as such, did not. He cared
about literary style, but he neither cared nor
knew about history. The following considerations will make this clear.

Euripides was, more than any other figure
in ancient history, a constant butt for the
attacks of comedy. And we find, oddly
enough, that most of the anecdotes about
Euripides in Satyrus are simply the jokes of

comedy treated as historical fact. For instance, in Aristophanes' play, *The Women at
the Thesmophoria*, the women, while alone
at this private festival, agree to murder
Euripides because, by his penetrating study
of female character on the stage, he has made
life too difficult for them. Euripides, hearing of the plot, persuades his elderly father-
in-law to go in disguise to the forbidden
celebration and defend him—which he does
in a ruinously tactless way. Some scenes of
brilliant farce are succeeded by a solemn
truce between Euripides and the women of
Athens. It shows what our tradition is
worth when we find that both the "*Life and
Race*," and Gellius and Satyrus himself, give
as sober fact this story which we know—
and if we did not know could surely see—to
be comic invention. There is another class
of fabulous anecdote which plays an even
larger part in the Satyrus tradition. In
Aristophanes' *Frogs* (1.1048), in a scene
where Euripides is defending his plays against
the attacks of Aeschylus, there occurs the
chance suggestion that Euripides had learnt
from his own experience all the varied vil-
lanies of his wicked heroines. The idea
took root, and he is represented in the anecdotes as a deceived husband, like his own

Theseus or Proetus, and uttering lines suitable to the occasion out of his own tragedies; as having two wives at once, like his own Neoptolemus—one of them named Choirile, or "Piggy," and each of course worse than the other; as torn to pieces by hounds, like his own Actaeon, or by wild women, like his own Pentheus.

Something of this sort is possibly the origin of a famous joke about Euripides' mother, which runs through Aristophanes and is repeated as a fact in all the Lives. We know from Philochorus that it was not true. The joke is to connect her with chervil—a grassy vegetable which grew wild and was only eaten in time of famine—or with wild green-stuff in general, or simply to call her a greengrocer. It was also a joke to say anything about beet-root. (*Acharn.* 894, *Frogs* 942.) A man begs Euripides to bring

"A new-born chervil from thy mother's breast."
(*Acharn.* 478.)

Or we hear that

"Wild wrongs he works on women
Wild as the greens that waved about his cradle."
(*Thesm.* 455.)

When some one is about to quote Euripides his friend cries:

"Don't, don't, for God's sake!   Don't be-chervil me!"
(*Knights* 19.)

Now a much-quoted line from Euripides'
tragedy *Melanippe the Wise* runs: "It is
not my word but my mother's word"; and
we know that Melanippe, and still more her
mother, was an authority on potent herbs
and simples. Turn his heroine's mother into
his own mother and the potent herbs into
some absurd vegetable, and the fable is
made.

Setting aside this fog of misunderstanding
and reckless anecdote, let us try to make out
the method on which our best authority,
Philochorus, may have put together his account of Euripides. He had almost no
written materials; he had no collection of
letters and papers such as go to the making
of a modern biography. He could, however,
consult the public records of tragic perform-
ances as collected and edited by Aristotle
and his pupils and thus fix the dates of
Euripides' plays, especially his first and last
performance, his first victory, and the like.
He would also find a few public inscriptions
in which the poet's name was mentioned, for
the archives of that time were mostly en-
graved on stone and put up in public places.
There was also a portrait bust, authentic
though slightly idealized, taken in the poet's
old age, and showing the worn and beautiful

face, the thin hair, and the lips somewhat
fallen in. These sources would give him a
few skeleton facts; for anything more he
would have to depend on the accidental
memories that survived. If he wrote about
300–290 B.C. there was no one living who
could remember a man who died in 406.
But there might be men of seventy whose
fathers had spoken to Euripides and whose
grandfathers had known him well. Thus he
might with luck have struck some vein of
intimate and intelligent memory, which
would have helped us to understand the
great man. But he did not. The memories
are all about the poet's old age, and they
are all very external. We hear that he wore
a long beard and had moles on his face. He
lived very much alone, and hated visitors
and parties. He had a quantity of books
and could not bear women. He lived on
the island of Salamis in a cave which had
two openings and a beautiful view—a good
cave was probably more comfortable than
many a Greek house, so this may not have
been a great eccentricity—and there you
could see him "all day long, thinking to
himself and writing, for he simply despised
anything that was not great and high." It
is like the memories of a child, rather a puz-

zled child, watching the great man from a
distance.

Some few things come out clearly. He
lived in his last years with a small knot of
intimates. Mnesilochus, his wife's father—
or, perhaps, another Mnesilochus of the same
family—was a close friend. So was his servant or secretary, Cephisophon. We do not
hear of Socrates as an intimate: the two
owed a great debt to one another, and we
hear that Socrates never went to the theatre
except when Euripides had a play perform-
ing: to see a Euripides play he would even
stir himself so far as to walk all the way to
the Piraeus. But it is likely enough that
both men were too vivid and original, perhaps too much accustomed to dominate
their respective circles, to be quite comfortable in the same room. And we never find
Euripides conversing with Socrates in Plato's
dialogues.

Some of Euripides' older friends were by
this time driven out from Athens. The great
"Sophist," Protagoras, had read his famous
book, *On the Gods*, in Euripides' own house.
But he was now dead, drowned at sea, and
the poet's master, Anaxagoras, had died long
before. Some of the younger artists seem to
have found a friend in Euripides. There was

Timotheus, the young Ionian composer, who
—like most musicians of any originality—
was supposed to have corrupted the music of
the day by his florid style and bold inven-
tions. His first performance in Athens was
a mortifying failure, and we are told that the
passionate Ionian was on the point of killing
himself when the old poet came and en-
couraged him. He had only to hold fast,
and the people who now hissed would turn
and applaud.

One fact is especially clear, the restless
enmity of the comic writers. Of the eleven
comedies of Aristophanes which have come
down to us three are largely devoted to Euripides, and not one has managed altogether
to avoid touching him. I know of no parallel
to it in all the history of literature. Has
there ever again been a tragic poet, or any
poet, who so centred upon himself year after
year till he was nearly eighty the mocking
attention of all the popular wits? And how
was it that the Athenian public never tired
of this incessant poet-baiting, these incessant appeals to literary criticism in the midst
of farce? The attacks are sometimes rough
and vicious, sometimes acute and searching,
often enough they hide a secret admiration.
And the chief enemy, Aristophanes, must,

to judge from his parodies, have known a
large number of Euripides' ninety-two plays
by heart, and been at least half fascinated
by the object of his satire. However that
may be, the hostility of the comic writers
had evidently a general hostility behind it.
Our tradition states this definitely and the
persistency of the attacks proves it. You
cannot go on constantly deriding on the
stage a person whom your audience does not
wish derided. And the unpopularity of Euripides, as we shall see later, is not hard to
understand. The Satyrus tradition puts it
down to his personal aloofness and auster-
ity. He avoided society, and he "made no
effort to please his audience." So that at
least he did not soften by personal pleasantness the opposition they felt to his whole
view of life. It was not only that he was
utterly alienated from the War Party and
the mob leaders: here he only agreed with
Aristophanes. It was that he had pierced
through to a deeper stratum of thought, in
which most of the pursuits and ideals of the
men about him stood condemned. Socrates
reached the same plane, and they killed
Socrates.

It is somewhat harder to understand the
universal assumption of our authorities that

Euripides was a notorious castigator of the
female sex and that the women of Athens
naturally hated him. To us he seems an
aggressive champion of women; more aggressive, and certainly far more appreciative,
than Plato. Songs and speeches from the
Medea are recited to-day at suffragist meet-
ings. His tragic heroines are famous and
are almost always treated with greater interest and insight than his heroes. Yet not
only the ancients, but all critics up to the
last generation or so, have described him as
a woman-hater. What does it mean? Is
Aristophanes ironical, and are the scholiasts
and grammarians merely stupid? Or is
there some explanation for this extraordinary judgment?

I think the explanation is that the present
age is the first, or almost the first, that has
learned to treat its heroines in fiction as real
human beings, with what are called "mixed
characters." As lately as the time of Sir
Walter Scott, perhaps as lately as Dickens,
common convention demanded that a
heroine, if sympathetic, should be so free
from faults as to be almost without character. Ibsen's heroines, who were real
human beings studied with sympathy but
with profound sincerity, seemed to their

generation shocking and even horrible. All
through the ages the ideal of womanhood in
conventional fiction has mostly been of the
type praised by one great Athenian thinker:
"the greatest glory for a woman is to be as
little mentioned as possible among men."
If that ideal was really predominant among
the women of Athens, it is no wonder that
they felt outraged by Euripides. They had
not reached, and most of their husbands
had not reached, the point of being interested
in good study of character, much less the
point of demanding a freer and more strenu-
ous life. To the average stupid Athenian it
was probably rather wicked for a woman to
have any character, wicked for her to wish
to take part in public life, wicked for her to
acquire learning, or to doubt any part of the
conventional religion, just as it was wicked
for her to deceive her husband. Such women
should not be spoken about; above all they
should not be treated with understanding
and sympathy. The understanding made it
all infinitely worse. To people of this type
the women of Euripides must have been
simply shocking and the poet himself a
cruel enemy of the sex. One only wonders
that they could stand Sophocles' heroines,
such as Antigone and Jocasta. To cleverer

men, like Aristophanes, the case would, no
doubt, seem rather more complicated. But
Aristophanes, amid the many flashes of
sympathy he shows for "advanced" women,
was not the man to go against his solid
conservative audience or to forgo such rich
material for jokes.

In any case this is the kind of picture we
have of Euripides in his last years; a figure
solitary, austere, with a few close intimates,
wrapped up in living for what he would call
"the service of the Muses," in music, poetry
and speculation; capable still of thrilling
his audiences with an intensity of tragic
emotion such as no other poet had ever
reached; but bowed with age, somewhat
friendless, and like other solitaries a little
strange in his habits; uncomprehendingly
admired and hated, and moving always
through a mist of half-envious, half-derisive
laughter. *Calvus et calvinista*—one is reminded, amid many differences, of the
quaint words in which William the Silent
describes his own passage from youth to age,
till the brilliant Catholic prince, leader of
courts and tourneys, sate at last in his
lonely council chamber "bald and a Cal-
vinist." Let us try to trace the path of
life which led him to this end.

He was the son of Mnesarchus or Mnesar-
chides—such names often have alternative
forms—who is said to have been a merchant.
His mother, Cleito, the supposed greengrocer,
was, according to Philochorus, "of very high
birth." He was born at Phlya, a village in
the centre of Attica. The neighbourhood is
celebrated still for its pleasant trees and
streams in the midst of a sunburnt land. In
Euripides' time it was more famous for its
temples. It was the seat of Demeter Anesi-
dora (Earth, Upsender of Gifts), of Dionysus
of the Blossom, and the Dread Virgins, old-
world and mysterious names, not like the
prevailing gods of the Homeric mythology.
Most famous of all, it possessed the mystery
temple of Erôs, or Love. Owing to the re-
searches of recent years, these mysteries
can now be in their general nature understood. They are survivals of an old tribal
society, in which all the boys as they reached
maturity were made to pass through certain
ordeals and initiations. They were connected
both with vegetation and with re-birth after
death, because they dated from a remote age
in which the fruitfulness of the tribal fields
was not differentiated from the fruitfulness of
the flocks and the human families, and the
new members born into the community were

normally supposed to be the old ancestors
returning to their homes. By Euripides'
day such beliefs had faded into mystical
doctrines, to be handled with speechless
reverence, not to be questioned or understood, but they had their influence upon his
mind. There were other temples, too, belong-
ing to the more aristocratic gods of heroic
mythology, as embodied in Homer. Euripides was in his youth cup-bearer to a certain
guild of Dancers—dancing in ancient times
had always religious associations about it
—who were chosen from the "first families
in Athens" and danced round the altar of
the Delian Apollo. He was also Fire-bearer
to the Apollo of Cape Zôstêr; that is, it was
his office to carry a torch in the procession
which on a certain night of each year met the
Delian Apollo at Cape Zôstêr, and escorted
him on his mystic path from Delos to Athens.

When the child was four years old he had
to be hurried away from his home and then
from his country. The Persians were coming.
The awful words lost none of their terror from
the fact that in Greek the word "Persai,"
Persians, meant "to destroy." So later it
added something to the dread inspired by
Rome that her name, "Roma," meant
"strength." The family must have crossed

the narrow seas to Salamis or further, and
seen the smoke of the Persian conflagrations
rising daily from new towns and villages of
Attica and at last from the Acropolis, or
Citadel, itself. Then came the enormous
desperate sea-battle; the incredible victory;
the sight of the broken oriental fleet beating
sullenly away for Asia and safety, and the
solemn exclamation of the Athenian general,
Themistocles, "It is not we who have done
this!" The next year the Athenians could
return to Attica and begin to build up their
ruined farms. Then came the final defeat of
the Persian land army at Plataea, and the
whole atmosphere lifted. Athens felt that
she had acted like a hero and was reaping a
hero's reward. She had borne the full brunt
of the war; she had voluntarily put herself
under the orders of Sparta rather than risk
a split in the Greek forces; and now she
had come out as the undisputed mistress of
the sea, the obvious champion round whom
the eastern Greeks must rally. Sparta,
not interested in matters outside her own
borders, and not capable of any constructive
policy, dropped sulkily out, and left her to
carry on the offensive war for the liberation
of the Greeks in Asia. The current of things
was with her.

But this great result was not merely the triumph of a particular city; it was the triumph of an ideal and a way of life. Freedom had defeated despotism, democracy had defeated kings, hardy poverty had defeated all the gold of the East. The men who fought of their free will for home and country had proved more lasting fighters than the conscripts who were kept in the lines by fear of tortures and beheadings and impalements. Above all "virtue," as the Greeks called it, or "virtue" and "wisdom" together, had shown their power. The words raise a smile in us; indeed, our words do not properly correspond with the Greek, because we can not get our ideas simple enough. "Virtue" is what makes a man, or anything else, good; it is the quality of a good soldier, a good general, a good citizen, a good bootmaker, a good horse or almost a good sword. And "wisdom" is that by which a man knows how to do things—to use a spear, or a tool, to think and speak and write, to do figures and history and geometry, to advise and convince his fellow-citizens. All these great forces moved, or so it seemed at the time, in the same direction; and probably it was hardly felt as a dangerous difference when many people preferred to say that it was "piety" that had won in the war against "impiety," and that the Persians had been destroyed because, being monotheists, they had denied the Gods. No doubt "piety," properly understood, was a kind of "wisdom." Let us take a few passages from the old Ionian historian, Herodotus, to illustrate what the feeling for Athens was in Euripides' youth.

Athens represented Hellenism (*Hdt.* I. 60). "The Greek race was distinguished of old from the barbarian as more intelligent and more emancipated from silly nonsense (or 'savagery') . . . And of all the Greeks the Athenians were counted first in Wisdom." Athens, as the old epigram put it, was "The Hellas of Hellas."

And this superior wisdom went with freedom and democracy. "So Athens grew. It is clear wherever you test it, what a good thing is equality among men. Athens under the tyrants was no better than her neighbours, even in war; when freed from the tyrants she was far the first of all." (V. 78.)

And what did this freedom and democracy mean? A speaker in Herodotus tells us (III. 80): "A tyrant disturbs ancient laws, violates women, kills men without trial. But a people ruling—first the very name of it is beautiful, and secondly a people does none of these things."

And the freedom is not mere licence. When Xerxes heard the small numbers of the Greeks who were opposed to him he asked why they did not all run away, "especially as you say they are free and there is no one to stop them?" And the Spartan answered: "They are free, O King, but not free to do everything. For there is a master over them named Law, whom they fear more than thy servants fear thee." (VII. 104. This refers specially to the Spartans, but the same tale is told by Aeschylus of the Athenians. It applies to any free Greeks as against the enslaved barbarian.)

The free Athenian must also have *aretê*, "virtue." He must be a better man in all senses than the common herd. As Themistocles put it; at every turn of life there is a choice between a higher and a lower, and they must choose the higher always. Especially there is one sense in which Athens must profess *aretê;* the sense of generosity or chivalry. When the various Greek states were contending for the leadership before the battle of Artemisium, the Athenians, though contributing much the largest fleet, "thought that the great thing was that Greece should be saved,

and gave up their claims." (*Hdt.* VIII. 3.)
In the similar dispute for the post of honour
and danger, before the battle of Plataea, the
Athenians did plead their cause and won it.
But they pleaded promising to abide loyally
by Sparta's decision if their claims were
rejected, and their arguments show what
ideal they had formed of themselves. They
claim that in recent years they alone have met
the Persians single-handed on behalf of all
Greece; that in old times it was they who
gave refuge to the children of Heracles when
hunted through Greece by the tyrant Eurystheus; it was they who, at the cost of war,
prevented the conquering Thebans from leaving their dead enemies to rot unburied and
thus offending against the laws of Greece and
humanity.

This is the light in which Athens conceived
herself; the ideal up to which, amid much confused, hot-headed and self-deceiving patriotism, she strove to live. She was to be the
Saviour of Hellas.

Euripides was about eight when the ruined
walls of Athens were rebuilt and the city,
no longer defenceless against her neighbours,
could begin to rebuild the "House of Athena"
on the Acropolis and restore the Temples and

the Festivals throughout Attica. He can hardly have been present when the general Themistocles, then at the height of his fame, provided the Chorus for the earliest of the great tragedians, Phrynichus, in 476 B.C. But he must have watched the new paintings being put up by the same Themistocles in the temples at Phlya, with scenes from the Persian War. And through his early teens he must have watched the far more famous series of pictures with which Polygnôtus, the first of the great Greek painters, was adorning the Acropolis; pictures that canonized scenes from the Siege of Troy and other legendary history. When he was ten he may probably have seen a curious procession which brought back from the island of Skyros the bones of Theseus, the mythical king of Athens and the accepted symbol, king though he was, of Athenian enlightenment and democracy. Athens was now too great and too self-conscious to allow Theseus to lie on foreign soil. When he was twelve he may have seen Aeschylus' *Persae*, "the one great play dealing with an historical event that exists in literature." When he was seventeen he pretty certainly saw the *Seven against Thebes* and was much influenced by it; but the Choregus this time was a new statesman, Pericles. Themistocles

was in banishment; and the other great heroes
of the Persian time, Aristides and Miltiades,
dead.

Next year, 466 B.C., Euripides became officially an "Ephêbus," or "Youth." He was
provided with a shield and spear, and set to
garrison and police duty in the frontier forts
of Attica. Full military service was to follow
in two years. Meantime the current of his
thoughts must have received a shock. For,
while his shield and spear were still fresh,
news came of one of the most stunning military disasters in Athenian history. A large
colony which had been established on the
river Strymon in Thrace had been lured into
dangerous country by the Thracian tribes,
then set upon by overwhelming numbers and
massacred to the number of ten thousand.
No wonder that one of Euripides' earliest
plays, when he took to writing, was the story
of *Rhesus*, the Thracian, and his rushing
hordes of wild tribesmen.

But meantime Euripides had not found
his work in life. We hear that he was a
good athlete; there were records of his prize-
winning in Athens and in Eleusis. Probably
every ambitious boy in Greece did a good deal
of running and boxing. More serious was his
attempt at painting. Polygnotus was at work

in Athens, and the whole art advancing by leaps and bounds. He tried to find his true work there, and paintings by his hand were discovered by antiquarians of later times—or so they believed—in the town of Megara. His writings show a certain interest in painting here and there, and it is perhaps the painter in him that worked out in the construction of his dramas such fine and varied effects of grouping.

But there was more in the air than painting and sculpture. The youth of Euripides fell in an age which saw perhaps the most extraordinary intellectual awakening known to human history. It had been preparing for about a century in certain cities of Ionian Greece, on the coast of Asia Minor, rich and cultivated states, subject for the most part to Lydian or Persian governors. The revolt of these cities and its suppression by Persia had sent numbers of Ionian "wise men," philosophers, poets, artists, historians, men of science, to seek for refuge in Greece, and especially in Athens. Athens was held to be the mother-city of all the Ionian colonies, and had been their only champion in the revolt. She became now, as one of these Ionian exiles put it, "the hearth on which the fire of Hellas burned." It is difficult to describe this great

movement in a few pages, but one can, perhaps, get some idea of it by an imaginary
comparison. Imagine first the sort of life
that was led in remote parts of Yorkshire or
Somerset towards the end of the eighteenth
century, a stagnant rustic life with no moving
ideas, and unquestioning in its obedience to
authority, in which hardly any one could read
except the parson, and the parson's reading
was not of a kind to stir a man's pulse. And
next imagine the intellectual ferment which
was then in progress in London or Paris; the
philosophers, painters, historians and men of
science, the voices proclaiming that all men
were equal, that the laws of England were unjust to the poor, that slavery was a crime,
and that monarchy was a false form of government, or that no action was morally wrong
except what tended to produce human misery.
Imagine then what would occur in the mind
of a clever and high-thinking boy who was
brought suddenly from the one society into
the heart of the second, and made to realise
that the battles and duties and prizes of life
were tenfold more thrilling and important
·than he had ever dreamed. That is the kind
of awakening that must have occurred in the
minds of a large part of the Greek people in
the early fifth century.

A thoroughly backward peasant in a Greek village—even an Attic village like Phlya—had probably as few ideas as other uneducated peasants. In Athens some fifty years later we hear that it was impossible, with the best will in the world, to find any one who could not read or write. (*Ar. Knights* 188 ff.) But the difference in time and place is cardinal. The countryman who voted for the banishment of Aristides the Just had to ask some one else to write the name for him. Such a man did not read nor yet think. He more or less hated the next village and regarded its misfortunes as his own advantage. He was sunk in superstition. His customs were rigid and not understood. He might worship a goddess with a horse's head or a hero with a snake's tail. He would perform for the welfare of his fields traditional sacrifices that were often filthy and sometimes cruel. On certain holy days he would tear small beasts to pieces or drive them into a fire; in very great extremities he would probably think no medicine so good as human blood. His rules of agriculture would be a mixture of rough common sense and stupid taboos: he would not reap till the Pleiades were rising, and he would carefully avoid sitting on a fixed stone. When

he sought for learning, he would get it in
old traditional books like *Hesiod*, which
taught him how Ouranos had been mutilated
by his son Cronos, and Cronos bound with
chains by his son Zeus; how Zeus was king
of gods and men, but had been cheated by
Prometheus into accepting bones instead of
meat in a sacrifice. He would believe that
Tantalus had given the gods his son Pelops
to eat, to see if they would know the difference, and some of them had eaten bits of
him. He would perhaps be ready, with
great hesitation, to tolerate certain timid at-
tempts to expurgate the story, like Pindar's,
for instance, which results, according to our
judgment, in making it rather worse. And
this man, rooted in his customs, his superstitions, his narrow-minded cruelties, will of
course regard every departure from his own
way of life as so much pure wickedness. In
every contest that goes on between Intelligence and Stupidity, between Enlightenment and Obscurantism, the powers of the
dark have this immense advantage: they
never understand their opponents, and consequently represent them as always wrong,
always wicked, whereas the intelligent party
generally makes an effort to understand the
stupid and to sympathize with anything

that is good or fine in their attitude. Many
of our Greek Histories still speak as if the
great spiritual effort which created fifth
century Hellenism was a mass of foolish
chatter and intellectual trickery and personal self-indulgence.

It was not that, nor anything like that.
Across the mind of our stupid peasant the
great national struggle against Persia brought
first the idea that perhaps really it was better
to die than to be a slave; that it was well to
face death not merely for his own home but
actually—incredible as it seemed—for other
people's homes, for the homes of those
wretched people in the next village. Our
own special customs and taboos, he would
reflect with a shiver, do not really matter
when they are brought into conflict with a
common Hellenism or a common humanity.
There are greater things about us than we
knew. There are also greater men. These
men who are in everybody's mouth: Themistocles above all, who has defeated the Persian and saved Greece: but crowds of others
besides, Aristides the Just and Miltiades, the
hero of Marathon; Demokêdes, the learned
physician, who was sought out by people in
need of help from Italy to Susa; Hecataeus,
who had made a picture of the whole earth,

showing all the countries and cities and
rivers and how far each is from the next,
and who could have saved the Ionians if
they had only listened to him; Pythagoras,
who had discovered all about numbers and
knew the wickedness of the world and had
founded a society, bound by strict rules, to
combat it. What is it about these men that
has made them so different from you and
me and the other farmers who meet in the
agora on market-day? It is *sophia*, wisdom;
it is *aretê*, virtue. They are not a bit stronger
in the arm, not bigger, not richer, or more
high-born: they are just wiser, and thus
better men. Cannot we be made wise? We
know we are stupid, we are very ignorant,
but we can learn.

The word Sophistes means either "one
who makes wise," or, possibly, as some
scholars think, "one who deals in wisdom."
The difference is slight. In any case it was
in answer to this call for *sophia* that the
Sophists arose. Doubtless they were of all
kinds; great men and small, honest and dis-
honest; teachers of real wisdom and of pre-
tence. Our tradition is rather bitter against
them, because it dates from the bitter time
of reaction and disappointment, when the
hopes of the fifth century and the men who

guided it seemed to have led Athens only to
her fall. Plato in particular is against them
as he is against Athens herself. In the main
the judgment of the afterworld upon them
will depend on the side we take in a never-
ending battle: they fought for light and
knowledge and freedom and the development of all man's powers. If we prefer
blinkers and custom, subordination and the
rod, we shall think them dangerous and
shallow creatures. But, to see what the
sophists were like, let us consider two of
them who are recorded as having specially
been the teachers of Euripides.

Anaxagoras of Clazomenae, in Ionia, was
about fifteen years older than Euripides, and
spent some thirty years of his life in Athens.
He discovered for the first time that the
moon shines by the reflection of the sun's
light; and he explained, in the main correctly,
the cause of eclipses. The sun was not a
god: it was a white-hot mass of stone or
earth, in size perfectly enormous. In describing its probable size, language failed
him; he only got as far as saying—what
must have seemed almost a mad exaggera-
tion—that it was many times larger than
the Peloponnese. He held, if he did not invent, a particular form of the atomic theory

which has played such a great rôle in the
history of modern science. He was emphatic
on the indestructibility of matter. Things
could be broken up into their elements and
could grow together again, but nothing
could be created or destroyed. There was
order in the world and purpose, and this
was the work of a conscious power which
he called "Nous," or Mind. "All things
were together in a mass, till Mind came and
put order into them." Mind is outside
things, not mixed with them, and some authorities say that Anaxagoras called it
"God." Meantime, he showed by experiment the reality and substance of air, and
disproved the common notion of "empty
space." It will be seen that these ideas, if
often crudely expressed, are essentially the
same ideas which gave new life to modern
science after the sleep of the Middle Ages.
Almost every one of them is the subject of
active dispute at the present day.

Apart from physical science, we learn that
Anaxagoras was a close friend and adviser
of the great Athenian statesman, Pericles;
and we have by chance an account of a long
discussion between the two men about the
theory of punishment—whether the object
of it is to do "justice" upon a wrong-doer

apart from any result that may accrue, or
simply to deter others from doing the same
and thus make society better. The question
is the subject of a vigorous correspondence
in the *Times* while these words are writing.
We can understand what an effect such a
teacher as this would have on the eager
young man from Phlya. One great word of
liberation was already in the air and belongs
to no one sophist or philosopher. This was
the distinction between Nature on the one
hand and Custom or Convention on the
other. The historian Herodotus, who was
no sophist but loved a good story, tells how
the Persian king, Darius, called some Greeks
and some Indian tribesmen together into
his presence. He then asked the Greeks
what payment would induce them to eat
the dead bodies of their fathers. "Nothing
in the world," they cried in indignation.
"They would reverently burn them." He
proceeded to ask the Indians what they
would take to burn their fathers' bodies,
and they repelled the bare thought with
horror; they would do nothing but eat them
with every mark of love and respect. "Fire
burns in the same way both here and in
Persia," the saying was, "but men's notions
of right and wrong are not at all the same."

The one is Nature; the other is man's Custom or Convention. This antithesis between "Phusis" and "Nomos" ran vividly through the whole of Greek philosophy, and awoke with renewed vigour in Rousseau and the radical writers of the eighteenth century. It is an antithesis against which conformist dialecticians have always turned their sharpest weapons. It has again and again been dissected and refuted and shown to be philosophically untenable: but it still lives and has still something of the old power to shatter and to set free. All the thinkers of Greece at the time we are treating were testing the laws and maxims of their day, and trying to find out what really rested on Nature and what was the mere embroidery of man. It is always a dangerous and exciting inquiry; especially because the most irrational conventions are apt also to be the most sacrosanct.

This whole spirit was specially incarnate in another of Euripides' teachers. We hear of Protagoras in his old age from that enemy of the sophists, Plato. But for this sophist even Plato's satire is kindly and almost reverent. Protagoras worked not at physical science, but at language and philosophy. He taught men to think and speak; he began the

study of grammar by dividing sentences into
four kinds, Optative, Interrogative, Indica-
tive, Imperative. He taught rhetoric; he
formulated the first theory of democracy.
But it was as a sceptic that he struck men's
imaginations most. "About the Gods, I
have no means of knowing either that they
are or are not. For the hindrances to knowledge are many, the darkness of the subject
and the shortness of man's life." Numbers
of people, no doubt, went as far as this, and
without suffering for it as Protagoras did;
but his scepticism cut deeper and raised
questions still debated in modern thought.
"Man is the measure of things"; there is no
truth to be had beyond the impression made
on a man's mind. When this given object
seems one thing to A and another thing to
B, it *is* to each one exactly what it seems;
just as honey not only seems sweet but *is*
sweet to a healthy man, and not only seems
bitter but *is* bitter to a man with jaundice.
Then you can not say, we may ask, that one
or other impression is false, and will prove
false on further inquiry? No: he answers;
each impression is equally true. The only
difference is that each state of mind is not
equally good. You cannot prove to the
jaundiced man that his honey is sweet, for

it is not: or to the drunkard that he does not
desire his drink, for he does: what you can
do is to alter the men's state of mind, to cure
the jaundice or the drunkenness. Our cogni-
tion flows and changes. It is the result of
an active impact upon a passive percipient.
And, resulting from this change, there are
in practice always two things to be said, a
pro and a con, about every possible proposi-
tion. There is no general statement that
cannot be contradicted. - ·. .

Other teachers also are represented as
having influenced Euripides; Archelaus, who
tried to conceive Anaxagoras' "Mind" in
some material form, as air or spirit—for
spiritus, of course, means "breath"; Pro-
dicus, who, besides his discoveries in grammar,
is the author of a popular and edifying fable
which has served in many schoolrooms for
many centuries. It tells how Heracles once
came to some cross roads, one road open,
broad, and smooth and leading a little down-
hill, the other narrow and uphill and rough:
and on the first you gradually became a
worse and worse man, on the second a better
one. There was Diogenes of Apollonia,
whose theories about air seem to have had
some effect on Euripides' writings; and of
course there was, among the younger men,

Socrates. Socrates is too great and too enigmatic a teacher to be summed up in a few sentences, and though a verse of ancient comedy has come down to us, saying, "Socrates piles the faggots for Euripides' fire," his influence in his older friend is not very conspicuous. Euripides must have caught something from his scepticism, his indifference to worldly standards, his strong purpose, and something also from his resolute rejection of all philosophy except that which was concerned with the doings and feelings of men. "The fields and trees will not talk to me; it is only the human beings in the city that will." That saying of Socrates might be the motto of many a dramatist.

The greatness of these philosophers or sophists of the fifth century does not, of course, lie in the correctness of their scientific results. The dullest and most unilluminated text-book produced at the present day is far more correct than Anaxagoras. Their greatness lies partly in the pioneer quality of their work. They first struck out the roads by which later workers could advance further. Partly in the daring and felicity with which they hit upon great and fruitful ideas, ideas which have brought light and

freedom with them whenever they have re-
curred to men's minds, and which, as we
have seen, are to a great extent still, after
more than two thousand years, living issues
in philosophic thought. Partly it lies in the
mere freedom of spirit with which they set
to work, unhampered by fears and taboos,
to seek the truth, to create beauty, and to
improve human life. The difference of atmosphere between the sophists of the Periclean circle and the ordinary backward Attic
farmer must have been visible to every
observer. If more evidence of the great gulf
was needed, it was supplied emphatically
enough in the experience of Euripides. He
was himself prosecuted by Cleon, the demagogue, for "impiety." The same charge had
been levelled even against his far less destructive predecessor, Aeschylus. Of these
three special friends whom we have mentioned, Euripides did not live to see Socrates
condemned to death and executed. But he
saw Anaxagoras, in spite of the protection of
Pericles, accused of "impiety" and compelled
to fly for his life. He saw Protagoras, for the
book which he had read aloud in Euripides'
own house, prosecuted and condemned. The
book was publicly burned; the author escaped, it is said, only to be drowned at sea, a

signal mark in the eyes of the orthodox of how the gods regarded such philosophy.

Thought was no doubt freer in ancient Athens than in any other city within two thousand years of it. Those who suffered for religious advance are exceedingly few. But it was not in human nature, especially in such early times, for individuals to do such great service to their fellow men and not occasionally be punished for it, They induced men for a time to set reason and high ideals above the instincts of the herd: and sooner or later the herd must turn and trample them.

One of the ancient lives says that it was this sense of the antagonism between Anaxagoras and the conservative masses that turned Euripides away from philosophy. One need scarcely believe that. The way he took was not the way to escape from danger or unpopularity. And when a man shows extraordinary genius for poetry one need not search for the reasons which induced him not to write prose. He followed in the wake not of Anaxagoras but of Aeschylus.

CHAPTER III

To the public of the present day a play is
merely an entertainment, and it was the same
to the Elizabethans. Shakespeare can say
to his audience, "Our true intent is all for
your delight," and we feel no particular
shock in reading the words. The companies
were just noblemen's servants; and it was
natural enough that if Lord Leicester's
players did not amuse Lord Leicester's guests,
they should be sent away and others hired.
If they too proved dull, the patron could
drop the play altogether and call for tum-
blers and dancing dogs.

To a playwright of the twelfth century,
who worked out in the church or in front of
it his presentation of the great drama of the
Gospel, such an attitude would have seemed
debased and cynical. However poor the
monkish players or playwright might be,

59

surely that which they were presenting was in itself enough to fill the mind of a spectator. To them, as the great mediævalist, Gaston Paris, puts it, "the universe was a vast stage, on which was played an eternal drama, full of tears and joy, its actors divided between heaven, earth and hell; a drama whose end is foreseen, whose changes of fortune are directed by the hand of God, yet whose every scene is rich and thrilling." The spectator was admitted to the councils of the Trinity; he saw the legions of darkness mingling themselves with the lives of humanity, tempting and troubling, and the saints and angels at their work of protection or intercession; he saw with his own eyes the kiss of Judas, the scourging and crucifixion, the descent into Hell, the resurrection and ascension; and, lastly, the dragging down to red and bloody torment of the infinite multitudes of the unorthodox or the wicked. Imagine what passed in the minds of those who witnessed in full faith such a spectacle! [*Poésie du Moyen Age I*, Essay I.]

Now, in spite of a thousand differences of social organization and religious dogma, the atmosphere of primitive Greek tragedy must have been most strangely similar to this. It is not only that, like the mediæval plays,

Greek tragedy was religious; that it was
developed out of a definite ritual; not even
that the most marked links of historical
continuity can be traced between the death-
and-resurrection ritual of certain Pagan
"saviours" and those of the mediæval
drama. It is that the ritual on which tragedy
was based embodied the most fundamental
Greek conceptions of life and fate, of law
and sin and punishment.

When we say that tragedy originated in a
dance, ritual or magical, intended to represent the death of the vegetation this year and
its coming return in triumph next year, the
above remarks may seem hard to justify.
But we must remember several things. First
a dance was in ancient times essentially religious, not a mere capering with the feet but
an attempt to express with every limb and
sinew of the body those emotions for which
words, especially the words of simple and un-
lettered men, are inadequate (see p. 227).
Again, vegetation is to us an abstract common noun; to the ancient it was a personal
being, not "it" but "He." His death was
as our own deaths, and his re-birth a thing
to be anxiously sought with prayers and
dances. For if He were not re-born, what
would happen? Famine, and wholesale death

by famine, was a familiar thought, a regularly returning terror, in these primitive
agricultural villages. Nay, more, why must
the cycle of summer and winter roll as it
does? Why must "He" die and men die?
Some of the oldest Greek philosophers have
no doubt about the answer: there has been
"Hubris" or "Adikia," Pride or Injustice,
and the result thereof must needs be death.
Every year He waxes too strong and commits
"Hubris," and such sin has its proper punishment. "The sun shall not transgress his
measures," says Heraclitus; "if he does he
shall be pursued by Erinyes, till justice be
re-fulfilled." It is the law of all existing
things. "They all pay retribution for injustice, one to another, according to the Or-
dinance of Time" (*Heraclitus*, fr. 94, *Anaxi-
mander*, fr. 9). And the history of each
year's bloom was an example of this refluent
balance. The Year Daemon—Vegetation
Spirit or Corn God or whatever we call him
—waxes proud and is slain by his enemy,
who becomes thereby a murderer and must
in turn perish at the hands of the expected
avenger, who is at the same time the Wronged
One re-risen. The ritual of this Vegetation
Spirit is extraordinarily widespread in all
quarters of the globe, and may best be

studied in Dr. Frazer's *Golden Bough,* especially in the part entitled, "*The Dying God.*" Dionysus, the daemon of tragedy, is one of these Dying Gods, like Attis, Adonis, Osiris.

The Dionysiac ritual which lay at the back of tragedy, may be conjectured in its full form to have had six regular stages: (1) an Agôn or Contest, in which the Daemon fights against his enemy, who—since it is really this year fighting last year—is apt to be almost identical with himself; (2) a Pathos, or disaster, which very commonly takes the shape of a "Sparagmos," or Tearing in pieces; the body of the Corn God being scattered in innumerable seeds over the earth; sometimes of some other sacrificial death; (3) a Messenger, who brings the news; (4) a Lamentation, very often mixed with a Song of Rejoicing, since the death of the Old King is also the accession of the new; (5) the Discovery or Recognition of the hidden or dismembered god; and (6) his Epiphany or Resurrection in glory.[1]

---

[1] The above is the present writer's re-statement, published in Miss Harrison's *Themis,* pp. 341 ff., of the orthodox view of the origin of tragedy. See also Cornford, *From Religion to Philosophy,* first few chapters. The chief non-Dionysiac theory is Professor Ridgeway's, who derives tragedy directly from the funeral cult of individual heroes: *Origin of Tragedy,* Cambridge, 1910.

This ritual of Dionysus, being made into a
drama and falling into the hands of a remarkable set of creative artists, developed
into what we know as Greek tragedy. The
creative passion of the artist gradually conquered the emotion of the mere worshipper.

Exactly the same development took place
in mediæval drama, or rather it was taking
place when new secular influences broke in
and destroyed it. The liturgical plays first
enacted the main story of the New Testa-
ment; then they emphasized particular parts
—there is a beautiful play, for instance, on
the Massacre of the Innocents; then they
developed imaginatively scenes that are
implied but not mentioned in the Gospel,
such as the experiences of the Magdalen
when she lived "in joy," her dealings with
cosmetic-sellers and the like; then, ranging
right outside the Gospel histories, they dealt
with the lives of St. Nicholas, St. Anthony
or any person who provided a good legend
and had some claim to an atmosphere of
sanctity.

In the same way Greek tragedy extended
its range first to embrace the histories of
other Heroes or Daemons—the difference is
slight—who were essentially like Dionysus:
Pentheus, Lycurgus, Hippolytus, Actaeon

and especially, I should be inclined to add,
Orestes. Then it took in any heroes to whose
memory some ritual was attached. For the
play is, with the rarest and most doubtful
exceptions, essentially the enactment of a
ritual, or rather of what the Greeks called
an "aition"—that is, a supposed historical
event which is the origin or "cause" of the
ritual. Thus the death of Hippolytus is the
"aition" of the lamentation-rite performed
at the grave of Hippolytus; the death of
Aias is the "aition" of the festival called
Aianteia; the death of Medea's children,
the "aition" of a certain ritual at Corinth;
the story of Prometheus the "aition" of a
certain Fire-festival in Athens. The tragedy,
as ritual, enacts its own legendary origin.

There is then a further extension of the
theme, to include a very few events in recent
history. But we must observe that only
those events were chosen which were felt to
have about them some heroic grandeur or
mystery; I think we may even say, only
those events which, like the Battle of Salamis
or the Fall of Miletus, had been made the
subject of some religious celebration.

However that may be, the general temper
of tragedy moved strongly away from the
monotony of fixed ritual. The subjects thus

grew richer and more varied; the mode of representation loftier and more artistic. What had begun as almost pure ritual ended by being almost pure drama. By the time Euripides began to write the master-trage-dian Aeschylus had already lifted Greek drama to its highest level: whole generations have read his plays without even suspect-ing. the ritual form that lies behind them. Aeschylus had also made the whole perform-ance much longer and more impressive: he composed three continuous tragedies form-ing a single whole and followed by the strange performance called a Satyr-play. The wild element of revelry which was proper to Dionysus worship, with its bearded dancing half-animal satyrs, had been kept severely away from the stage during the three tragedies and must burst in to have its fling when they were finished. The other tragedians do not seem to have written in trilogies, and Euripides at any rate moved gradually away from satyr-plays. In their stead he put a curious sort of pro-satyric tragedy, a play in the tragic convention and free from the satyric courseness, but con-taining at least one half-comic figure and preserving some fantastic quality of at-mosphere.

On the Great Festival of Dionysus each
year—and sometimes on other festivals—
this ritual of tragedy was solemnly performed
in the theatre of the god. Like most Greek
festivals the performance took the form of a
competition. The ground of this custom was,
I suspect, religious. It was desired to get a
spirit of "Nikê," or victory, into the celebration, and you could only get this by means of
a contest. The Archon, or magistrate, in
charge of the festival selected three poets to
compete, and three rich men to be their
"Chorêgoi," that is, to provide all the ex-
penses of the performance. The poet was
then said to have "obtained a chorus," and
his work now was to "teach the chorus." At
the end of the festival a body of five judges,
somewhat elaborately and curiously chosen,
awarded a first, second and third prize. Even
the last competitor must have a kind of
"victory"; any mention of "failure" at
such a time would be ill-omened.

This, in rough outline, was the official
mould in which our poet's creative activity
had to run. The record of his early work is,
as we had reason to expect, terribly defective. But we do happen to know the name
and subject of the first play for which he
"was granted a chorus." It was called the

Daughters of Pelias. Its story was based on
the old ritual of the Year-god, who is cut
to pieces or scattered like the seed, and then
restored to life and youth. Medea, the en-
chantress maiden from the further shores of
the Friendless Sea, had fled from her home
with the Greek adventurer Jason, the winner
of the Golden Fleece. She came with him
to Thessaly, where his uncle Pelias was king.
Pelias had usurped Jason's ancestral crown
and therefore hated him. The daughters of
Pelias doubtless sneered at Medea and en-
couraged Jason's growing distaste for his
barbarian prize. The savage woman determined at one blow to be rid of Pelias, to
punish his daughters, and reconquer Jason's
love. She had the power of renovating the
life of the old. She persuaded the daughters
of Pelias to try her method on their father,
with the result that he died in agony, and
they stood guilty of a hideous murder.
Medea, we may conjecture, was triumphant,
till she found she had made Jason a ruined
man and taught him really to hate her. The
play is characteristic in two ways. It was
clearly based on the old ritual, and it treated
one of Euripides' great subjects, the passions
of a suffering and savage woman.

The *Daughters of Pelias* was produced in

455, when the poet was twenty-nine, just a year after the death of Aeschylus and thirteen years after the first victory of Sophocles. Euripides' own first victory—we do not know the name of the successful play—did not come till 442, a year before Sophocles' masterpiece, the *Antigone*.

We have only two examples, and those not certain, of Euripides' work before that time. The *Cyclops* is a satyr-play pure and simple, and the only complete specimen of its class. It is probably earlier than the *Alcestis*, and is interesting because it shows Euripides writing for once without any *arrière pensée*, or secondary intention. It is a gay and grotesque piece, based on Homer's story of Odysseus in the Cyclops' cave. The farcical and fantastic note is firmly held, so that the climax of the story, in which the monster's eye is burnt out with a log of burning wood, is kept unreal and not disgusting. The later Euripides would probably have made it horrible and swung our sympathies violently round to the side of the victim.

The *Rhesus* has come down to us in a very peculiar condition and is often considered spurious. We know, however, that Euripides wrote a *Rhesus*, and tradition says that he was "very young" when he wrote

it. My own view—explained in the preface
to my translation—would make it probably
a very early pro-satyric play which was
produced after the poet's death and considerably rewritten. It is a young man's play,
full of war and adventure, of spies in wolf-
skins and white chargers and gallant chivalry.
That is not much like the Euripides whom
we know elsewhere; but his mark is upon the
last scene, in which the soldiers stand em-
barrassed and silent while a solitary mother
weeps over her dead son. The poetry of the
scene is exquisite; but what is most characteristic is the sudden flavour of bitterness,
the cold wind that so suddenly takes the
heart out of joyous war. Some touch of
that bitter flavour will be found hereafter in
every play, however beautiful or romantic,
that comes from the pen of Euripides.

Up to the year 438, when the poet was
forty-six, the records, as we have said, almost
fail us. But in that year he produced a set
of four plays, *The Cretan Women, Alcmaeon
in Psôphis, Telephus*, and, in place of a
satyr-play, the *Alcestis*. The last is still extant and is very characteristic of the master's
mind. The saga told how Admetus, a king
in Thessaly, was fated to die on a certain
day, but, in return for his piety of old, was

allowed to find a substitute to die for him.
His old father and mother refused; his young
wife, Alcestis, gladly consented to die.
Amid exquisite songs of mourning she is
carried to her grave, when the wild hero,
Heracles, comes to the house seeking hos-
pitality. Admetus, with primitive courtesy,
conceals what has happened and orders him
to be given entertainment. The burial is
finished when Heracles, already revelling
and drunken and crowned with flowers,
learns the truth. Sobered at the touch he
goes out into the night to wrestle with Death
amid the tombs and crush his ribs for him
till he yields up his prey. One sees the fantastic satyr note. The play is not truly
tragic; it touches its theme tenderly and
with romance. But amid all the romance
Euripides cannot keep his hand from un-
veiling the weak spot in the sacred legend.
Alcestis, no doubt, is beautiful, and it was
beautiful of her to die. But what was it of
Admetus to let her die? An ordinary playwright would elude the awkward question.
Admetus would refuse his wife's sacrifice
and she would perform it against his will or
without his knowledge. We should somehow
save our hero's character. Not so Euripides.
His Admetus weeps tenderly over his wife,

but he thinks it entirely suitable that she
should die for him. The veil is not removed
from his eyes till his old father, Pheres, who
has bluntly refused to die for anybody,
comes to bring offerings to Alcestis' funeral.
A quarrel breaks out between the two selfish
men, brilliantly written, subtle and merci-
less, in which Admetus' weakness is laid
bare. The scene is a great grief to the
purely romantic reader, but it just makes
the play profound instead of superficial.

All the plays of 438 are, in different ways,
typical of their author. And we will spend
a little time on each. The *Alcmaeon in
Psôphis* was what we should call a romance.
Alcmaeon was the son of that Eriphyle who
betrayed her husband to death for the sake
of a charmed necklace which had once belonged to Harmonia, the daughter of Ares.
Alcmaeon slew his mother and became in
consequence mad and accursed. Seeking
purification he fled to the land of Psôphis,
where the king cleansed him and gave him
the hand of his daughter Arsinoë, who duly
received the necklace. However, Alcmaeon's
sin was too great for any such cleansing. He
wandered away, all the earth being accursed
to him, till he should find some land that had
not been in existence at the time of his sin

and was consequently unpolluted. He discovered it in some alluvial islands, just then
making their appearance at the mouth of
the River Achelotis. Here he at last found
peace and married the daughter of Achelotis,
Callirrhoë. She asks for the necklace and
Alcmaeon goes back to get it from Arsinoë.
He professes to need it for his own
purification and she willingly gives it him;
then she finds that he really wants it for
his new bride, and in fury has him
murdered on his road home. A romantic
and varied story with one fine touch of
tragic passion.

The *Telephus* also deserves special mention. It had apparently the misfortune to
be seen by Aristophanes, then a boy about
sixteen. At any rate the comedian was never
able to forget it, and we know it chiefly from
his parodies. It struck out a new style in
Attic drama, the style of adventure and plot-
interest, which threw to the winds the traditional tragic dignities and pomps. The
usual convention in tragedy was to clothe
the characters in elaborate priestly dress
with ritual masks carefully graduated according to the rank of the character. Such
trappings came to Tragedy as an inherit-
ance from its old magico-religious days, and

it never quite succeeded in throwing them
off, even in its most vital period. It is very
difficult for us to form a clear notion what
the ordinary Greek tragedy looked like in
438, and how much we should have noticed
any great change of dressing in the *Telephus*.
But there was a change which raised a storm
of comment. Telephus was a King of Mysia,
not very far from the Troad. The Greeks
in sailing for Troy had missed their way and
invaded Telephus' country by mistake. He
had fought them with great effect but had
been wounded by Achilles with his magic
spear. The wound would not close, and an
oracle told Telephus "the wounder shall
heal." The Greeks were back in Greece by
this time, planning a new invasion of Troy.
The king goes, lame and disguised as a
beggar, into the heart of the Greek army
and into Agamemnon's palace. Euripides,
since the king had to be a beggar, dressed
him as a beggar, with rags and a wallet. It
is hard to see how he could possibly have
done otherwise, but we may surmise that
his beggar's dress was a little more realistic
and less merely symbolical than his audience expected. In any case, though critics
were shocked, the practice established itself.
Telephus and Philoctêtes were afterwards

regularly allowed to dress in "rags," even
in the work of Sophocles.

There were great scenes owing to the bold-
ness of the ragged and intrusive stranger.
The Greek chieftains proposed to kill him,
but granted him at last the right of making
one speech to save his life. He seems to
have spoken beside, or over, the headsman's
block. And the case he had to plead was
characteristic of Euripides. The Greeks
considered quite simply that Telephus was
their enemy and must be destroyed on their
next expedition. The beggar explained that
Telephus had found his country ravaged
and was bound to defend it. Every man
among the Greeks would have done the
same; there is nothing to blame Telephus
for. At the end of this scene, apparently,
the beggar was discovered. It is Telephus
himself speaking! They fly to their spears.
But Telephus has snatched up the baby
prince, Orestes, from his cradle and stands
at bay; if one of his enemies moves the child
shall die. Eventually they accept his terms
and make peace with him. A fine melodrama, one would guess, and a move in the
direction of realism—a direction which Euripides only followed within certain strict
limits. But we find two marks of Euripides

the philosopher. The beggar who pleads
for reasonable justice towards the national
enemy strikes a note which Euripides himself often had to sound afterwards. It was
not for nothing that Aristophanes in his
Acharnians, thirteen years later, used a
parody of this scene in order to plead the
dangerous cause of reasonableness towards
Sparta. The other mark is a curious tang
of sadness at the close. The Greeks demand
that Telephus, so brave and resourceful,
shall be their ally against Troy. But his
wife is a Trojan princess and he refuses.
He consents reluctantly to show the army
the road to his wife's fatherland and then
turns away.

The remaining play of the trilogy performed in 438 strikes a chord that proved
more dangerous to Euripides. The *Cretan
Women* told the story of Aëropê, a Cretan
princess who secretly loved a squire or
young soldier. Her intrigue is discovered,
and her father gives her to a Greek sailor
to throw into the sea. The sailor spares her
life and takes her to Greece. The story as
it stands is a common ballad motive and not
calculated to disturb any one. But the disciple of the sophists did not leave these romances where he found them. He liked to

think them out in terms of real life. The
songs in which Aëropê poured out her love
were remembered against Euripides after
his death. It was all very well to sympathize
in a remote artistic way with these erring
damsels; but Euripides seemed to come too
near raising an actual doubt whether the
damsel had done anything so very wrong
at all, that respectable people should want
to murder her. [Euripides is, as a matter of
fact, not loose but highly austere in his
moral tone. But next to religion itself, the
sphere of sexual conduct has always been the
great field for irrational taboos and savage
punishments, and the sophists naturally
marked it as a battle-field.] The kings of
Egypt commonly married their sisters, and
did so on religious grounds: to a Greek such
marriage was an unspeakable sin. There is
a problem here, and Euripides raised it
sharply in a play, *Aeolus*, based on the old
fairy-tale of the King of the winds who
dwells as a patriarch on his floating island
with his twelve sons married to his twelve
daughters. "Canst face mine eyes, fresh
from thy deed of shame?" says the angry
father in this play; and his son answers,
"What *is* shame, when the doer feels no
shame?" [Euripides also treated several

times legends where a god became the lover
of a mortal maiden, and, as we shall see in
the *Ion*, he loved to rouse sympathy for the
maiden and contempt for the god (p. 119).
In one case he even treats, through a mist
of strange religious mysticism, the impossible amour of Pasiphaë of Crete with the
Cretan Bull-god. It is interesting, however,
to observe that there is in Euripides no trace
of sympathy for the one form of perverted
indulgence on which the ancient tone was
markedly different from ours. It is reserved
for the bestial Cyclops and Laius the accursed.

Adventure, brilliance, invention, romance
and scenic effect; these together with de-
lightful lyrics, a wonderful command over
the Greek language, and a somewhat daring
admixture of sophistic wisdom which sometimes took away a spectator's breath, were
probably the qualities which the ordinary
public had felt in Euripides' work up to the
year 438. They perhaps felt also that these
pleasant gifts were apt to be needlessly
marred by a certain unintelligible note of
discord. It was a pity; and, as the man
was now forty-six, he ought surely to have
learnt how to smooth it out!

It was not smoothness that was coming.

CHAPTER IV

BEGINNING OF THE WAR: THE PLAYS OF
MATURITY, "MEDEA" TO "HERACLES"

THE next play of which we have full
knowledge must have staggered its audience. The *Medea* was promptly put by
the official judges at the bottom of the list
of competing plays, and thereafter took its
place, we do not know how soon, as one of
the consummate achievements of the Greek
tragic genius. Its stamp is fixed on all the
imagination of antiquity.

The plot of the *Medea* begins where that
of the *Daughters of Pelias* (p. 68) ended.
Jason had fled with Medea and her two
children to Corinth, which is ruled by Creon,
an old king with a daughter but no son to
succeed him. The famous warrior-prince will
just suit Creon as a son-in-law, if only he will
dismiss his discreditable barbarian mistress.
Jason has never been able to tell the truth
to Medea yet; who could? He secretly accepts Creon's terms; he marries the princess;

and Creon descends on Medea with soldiers
to remove her instantly from the territory
of Corinth. Medea begs for one day in
which to make ready for exile, for the children's sake. One day will be enough. By
desperate flattery and pleading she gets it.
There follows a first scene with Jason, in
which man and woman empty their hearts
on one another—at least they try to; but
even yet some fragments of old habit and
conventional courtesy prevent Jason from
telling the full truth. Still it is a wonderful
scene, Jason reasonable and cold, ready to
recognize all her claims and provide her with
everything she needs except his own heart's
blood; Medea desolate and half mad, asking
for nothing but the one thing he will not
give. Love to her is the whole world, to
him it is a stale memory. This scene ends
in defiance, but there is another in which
Medea feigns repentance and submission,
and sends Jason with the two children to
bear a costly gift to the new bride. It may,
she suggests, induce Creon to spare the
children and let her go to exile alone. The
gift is really a robe of burning poison, which
has come to Medea from her divine ancestor,
the Sun. The bride dies in agony together
with her father who tries to save her. Jason

rushes to save his two children from the vengeance which is sure to come upon them
from the kinsmen of the murdered bride;
but Medea has already slain them with her
own hand and stands laughing at him over
their bodies. She too suffers, but she loves
the pain, since it means that he shall
have happiness no more. The Daughter
of the Sun sails away on her dragon chariot
and an ecstasy of hate seems to blind the
sky.

The *Medea* shows a new mastery of tragic
technique, especially in the extraordinary
value it gets out of the chorus (p. 238). But
as illustrating the life of Euripides there are
one or two special points in it that claim
notice. In the first place it states the cause
of a barbarian woman against a Greek man
who has wronged her. Civilized men have
loved and deserted savage women since the
world began, and I doubt if ever the deserted
one has found such words of fire as Medea
speaks. The marvel is that in such white-
hot passion there is room for satire. But
there is; and even a reader can scarcely
withhold a bitter laugh when Jason explains
the advantage he has conferred on Medea by
bringing her to a civilized country. But
Medea is not only a barbarian; she is also

a woman, and fights the horrible war that lies, an eternally latent possibility, between woman and man. Some of the most profound and wounding things said both by Medea and by Jason might almost be labelled in a book of extracts "Any wife to any husband," or "Any husband to any wife." And Medea is also a witch; she is also at heart a maniac. It is the madness produced by love rejected and justice denied, by the sense of helpless, intolerable wrong. A lesser poet might easily have made Medea a sympathetic character, and have pretended that long oppression makes angels of the oppressed. In the great chorus which hymns the rise of Woman to be a power in the world it would have been easy to make the Woman's day a day of peace and blessing. But Euripides, tragic to the heart and no dealer in pleasant make-believe, saw things otherwise; when these oppressed women strike back, he seems to say, when these despised and enslaved barbarians can endure no longer, it will not be justice that comes but the revenge of madmen.

This kind of theme was not in itself likely to please an audience; but what always galls the average theatre-goer most in a new work of genius is not the subject but the

treatment. Euripides' treatment of his subject was calculated to irritate the plain man
in two ways. First it was enigmatic. He
did not label half his characters bad and half
good; he let both sides state their case and
seemed to enjoy leaving the hearer bewildered. And further, he made a point of study-
ing closely and sympathetically many regions
of thought and character which the plain
man preferred not to think of at all. When
Jason had to defend an obviously shabby
case, no gentleman cared to hear him; but
Euripides insisted on his speaking. He enjoyed tracking out the lines of thought and
feeling which really actuate men, even fine
men like Jason, in Jason's position. When
Medea was revealed as obviously a wicked
woman the plain man thought that such
women should simply be thrashed, not listened to. But Euripides loved to trace all
her complicated sense of injustice to its
origins, and was determined to understand
and to explain rather than to condemn.
The plain man had a kind of justification
for saying that Euripides actually seemed to
like these traitors and wicked women; for
such thorough understanding as this in-
volves always a good deal of sympathy.

This charge could with even more reason

be brought against another masterpiece of
drama, which followed three years after the
Medea. The *Hippolytus* (428 B.C.) did indeed win the first prize from the official
judges, besides establishing itself in the admiration of after ages and inspiring Seneca
and Racine to their finest work. But it pro-
foundly shocked public opinion at the same
time. The plot is a variant of a very old
theme found in ancient Egypt and in the
Pentateuch. Theseus, not here the ideal
democrat on the Athenian throne, but the
stormy and adventurous hero of the poets,
had early in life conquered the Amazons and
ravished their virgin Queen. She died, leaving a son like herself, Hippolytus. Theseus
some twenty years after married Phaedra,
the young daughter of Minos, king of Crete,
and she by the evil will of Aphrodite fell in
love with Hippolytus. She told no one her
love, and was trying to starve herself to
death, when her old nurse contrived to worm
the secret from her and treacherously, under
an oath of secrecy, told it to Hippolytus.
Phaedra, furious with the Nurse and with
Hippolytus, in a blind rage of self-defence,
writes a false accusation against Hippolytus
and hangs herself. Hippolytus, charged by
Theseus with the crime, will not break his

oath and goes out to exile under his father's
curse. The gods, in fulfilment of the curse,
send death to him, but before he actually
dies reveal his innocence. The story which
might so easily be made ugly or sensual is
treated by Euripides with a delicate and
austere purity. In construction, too, and
general beauty of workmanship, though not
in greatness of idea or depth of passion, the
Hippolytus is perhaps the finest of all his
plays, and has still a great appeal on the
stage. But the philistine was vaguely hurt
and angered by the treatment, so tender
and yet so inexorable, accorded to a guilty
love, and doubtless the more conventional
Athenian ladies shocked themselves over
the bare idea of such a heroine being mentioned. It gives us some measure of the
stupidity of public criticism at the time,
that we find special attacks made upon one
phrase of Hippolytus. In his first rage with
the Nurse he vows he will tell Theseus of
her proposal. She reminds him of his oath,
and he cries:

" 'T was but my tongue, 't was not my heart that swore."

It is a passing flash of indignation at the
trap in which he has been caught. When the
time comes he keeps his oath at the cost of

his life. Yet the line is repeatedly cited as
showing the dreadful doctrines of Euripides
and the sophists; doctrines that would justify any perjury!

The *Hippolytus*, as we have it, is a rewritten play. In his first version Euripides
had a scene in which Phaedra actually declared her love. This more obvious treatment was preferred by Seneca and Racine;
but Euripides in his second thoughts reached
a far more austere and beautiful effect. His
Phaedra goes to her death without having
spoken one word to Hippolytus: she has
heard him but has not answered. The
Hippolytus has more serene beauty than any
of Euripides' plays since the *Alcestis*, and is
specially remarkable as the first great drama
on the subject of tragic or unhappy love, a
theme which has been so extraordinarily
fruitful on the modern stage. To contemporaries it was also interesting as one of the
earliest treatments of a purely local Attic
story, which had not quite found its way
into the great sagas of epic tradition.

The note of the *Medea* was struck again
some two years later (426?) in a play almost
equally powerful and more horrible, the
Hecuba. The heroine is the famous Queen of
Troy, a barbarian woman like Medea, ma-

jestic and beautiful at the beginning of the
action and afterwards transformed by intolerable wrongs into a kind of devil. Her
"evils" are partly the ordinary evils that
come to the conquered in war, but they are
made worse by the callousness of her Greek
conquerors. The play strikes many notes of
special bitterness. For instance, the one
champion whom Hecuba finds among her
conquerors is the general, Agamemnon. He
pleads her cause in the camp, because, God
help him! he has taken her daughter Cassandra, the mad prophetess vowed to eternal
virginity, to be his concubine, and consequently feels good-natured. There is another
note, remarkable in an Athenian. The mob
of the Greek army, in a frenzy of superstition,
clamour to have a Trojan princess sacrificed
at Achilles' tomb. In the debate on this subject we are told that several princes spoke;
among them the two sons of Theseus, the
legendary kings of Athens. They would
surely, as enlightened Athenians, prevent
such atrocities? On the contrary, all we hear
is that they spoke against one another, but
both were for the murder! At the end of the
Hecuba, as at the end of the *Medea*, we are
wrought to a pitch of excitement at which
incredible legends begin to seem possible.

History related that the Queen of Troy, maddened by her wrongs, had been transformed into a kind of Hell-hound with fiery eyes, whom sailors saw at night prowling round the hill where she was stoned. In her bloody revenge on the only enemy she can trap into her power, she seems already to have become this sort of being in her heart, and when her blind and dying victim prophesies the coming transformation, it seems natural. One only feels that perhaps the old miraculous stories are true after all. The one light that shines through the dark fury of the *Hecuba* is the lovely and gentle courage, almost the joy, with which the virgin martyr, Polyxena, goes to her death.

I have taken the *Hecuba* slightly before its due date, because of its return with increased bitterness to the tone and subject of the *Medea*. We will now go back. There had been in the interim a change in the poet's mind, or, at the least, a strong clash of conflicting emotions. The *Medea* was produced in 431, the first year of the Peloponnesian War. This war, between the Athenian empire, representing the democratic and progressive forces of Greece, and the Peloponnesian confederacy with Sparta at its head, lasted with one interruption for twenty-seven years and ended in the capture of Athens and the destruction of her power. When war was first declared it represented the policy of Pericles, the great statesman of the Enlightenment, the friend of Anaxagoras, and of those whom Euripides honoured most. It seemed at first like a final struggle between the forces of progress and those of resolute darkness. Pericles in a famous speech, which is recorded for us by Thucydides, had explained to his adherents the great causes for which Athens stood; had proclaimed her as the Princess of Cities for whom it was a privilege to die; and urged them, using a word more vivid in Greek than it is in English, to stand about her like a band of Lovers round an Immortal Mistress. Euripides was as a matter of fact still going through his military service and must have seen much hard fighting in these first years of the war.

He responded to Pericles' call by a burst of patriotic plays. Even in the *Medea* there is one chorus, a little out of place perhaps, but famous in after days, describing the glories of Athens. They are not at all the conventional glories attributed by all patriots to their respective countries. "It is an old and happy land which no conqueror has ever subdued; its children walk delicately through air that

shines with sunlight; and Wisdom is the very
bread that they eat." (The word is "sophia,"
embracing Wisdom, Knowledge, Art, Culture; there is no one word for it in English,
and the names for the various parts of it
have lost their poetry.) "A river," he continues, "flows through the land; and legend
tells that Cypris, the Goddess of Love, has
sailed upon it and dipped her hand in the
water; and now when the river-wind at
evening blows it comes laden with a spirit
of longing; but it is not ordinary love, it is a
Passion and a great Desire for all kinds of
godlike endeavour, a Love that sits with
Wisdom upon her throne." . . . "A pity
the man should be so priggish." We may
imagine the comment of the average Athenian paterfamilias.

Towards the beginning of the war we may
safely date the *Children of Heracles*, a mutilated but beautiful piece, which rings with
this particular spirit of patriotism (cf. p. 41
above). Heracles is dead; his children and
mother are persecuted and threatened with
death by his enemy, Eurystheus, king of
Argos. Under the guidance of their father's
old comrade, Iolaus, they have fled from
Argos, and tried in vain to find protectors in
every part of Greece. No city dares protect

them against the power of Argos. At the opening of the play we find the children and Iolaus clinging as suppliants to an altar in Athens. The herald of Argos breaks in upon them, flings down the old man and prepares to drag the children off. "What hope can Iolaus possibly cherish?" Iolaus trusts in two things, in Zeus who will protect the innocent, and in Athens which is a free city and not afraid. The king of Athens, a son of Theseus, appears and rebukes the herald. The herald's argument is clear: "These children are Argive subjects and are no business of yours; further, they are utterly helpless and will be no possible good to you as allies. And if you do not give them up peacefully, Argos declares instant war." The king "wishes for peace with all men; but he will not offend God, nor betray the innocent; also he rules a free city and will take no orders from any outside power. As to the fate of these children not being his business, it is always the business of Athens to save the oppressed." One remembers the old claim, emphatically approved by the historian of the Persian Wars, that Athens was the saviour of Hellas. One remembers also the ultimatum of the Peloponnesian confederacy which Pericles rejected on the eve of the

present war; and the repeated complaints of
the Corinthians that Athens "will neither
rest herself nor let others rest." These supply
the clue to a large part of the patriotism of
the *Children of Heracles*. There is another
element also, and perhaps one that will better
stand the test of impartial criticism, in Euripides' ideal of Athens. She will be true to
Hellas and all that Hellas stands for: for law,
for the gods of mercy, for the belief in right
rather than force. Also, as the king of
Athens is careful to observe, for democracy
and constitutional government. He is no
despot ruling barbarians.

The same motives recur with greater fulness and thoughtfulness in another play of the
early war time—the exact year is not certain
—the *Suppliant Women*. Scholars reading
the play now, in cool blood, with the issues at
stake forgotten, are inclined to smile at a sort
of pedantry in the poet's enthusiasm. It
reminds one of the punctiliousness with which
Shelley sometimes gives one the sincere milk
of the word according to Godwin. This play
opens, like the last, with a scene of supplica-
tion. A band of women—Argive mothers
they are this time, whose sons have been slain
in war against Thebes—have come to Athens
as suppliants. They are led by Adrastus, the

great and conquered lord of Argos, and find-
ing Aethra, the king's mother, at her prayers
beside the altar, have surrounded her with a
chain of suppliant branches which she dares
not break. They only ask that Theseus, her
son, shall get back for them the bodies of
their dead sons, whom the Thebans, contrary
to all Hellenic law, have flung out unburied
for dogs to tear. Theseus at first refuses, on
grounds of policy, and the broken-hearted
women take up their branches and begin to
go, when Aethra, who has been weeping
silently, breaks out: "Is this kind of wrong
to be allowed to exist?"

> "Thou shalt not suffer it, thou being my child!
> Thou hast seen men scorn thy City, call her wild
> Of counsel, mad; thou hast seen the fire of morn
> Flash from her eyes in answer to their scorn.
> Come toil on toil; 't is this that makes her grand;
> Peril on peril! And common states, that stand
> In caution, twilight cities, dimly wise—
> Ye know them, for no light is in their eyes.
> Go forth, my son, and help. My fears are fled.
> Women in sorrow call thee, and men dead."
>
> (*Suppl.* 320 ff.)

Theseus accepts his mother's charge. It
has been his old habit to strike wherever he
saw oppression without counting the risk;
and it shall never be said of him that an
ancient Law of God was set at naught when

he and Athens had power to enforce it. It is
Athens as the "saviour of Hellas" that we
have here. It is Athens the champion of
Hellenism and true piety, but it is also the
Athens of free thought and the Enlightenment. For later on, when the dead bodies are
recovered from the battle-field, they are a
ghastly sight. The old unreflecting Greece
would in the first place have thought them a
pollution, a thing which only slaves must be
sent to handle. In the second place, since
the mothers were making lamentation, the
bodies must be brought to their eyes, so as to
improve the lamentation. But Theseus feels
differently on both points. Why should the
mothers' grief be made more bitter? Let the
bodies be burned in peace and the decent
ashes given to the mothers. And as to the
defilement, the king himself, we hear, has
taken up the disfigured bodies in his arms
and washed their wounds and "shown them
love."   No   slave   touched   them.   "How
dreadful! Was he not ashamed?" asks a
bystander—the Greek word means something between "ashamed" and "disgusted."
"No," is the answer: "Why should men be
repelled by one another's sufferings?" (768).
It is a far-reaching answer, with great conse-
quences. It is the antique counterpart of St.

Francis kissing the leper's sores. The man
of the herd is revolted by the sight of great
misery and inclines to despise and even hate
the sufferer; the man of the enlightenment
sees deeper, and the feeling of revulsion
passes away in the wish to help.

We spoke of a slight pedantry in the en-
thusiasms of the *Suppliant Women.* It is
illustrated even by points like this, and by
a tendency in Theseus to lecture on good
manners and the Athenian constitution. The
rude Theban herald enters asking, "Who
is monarch of this land?" using the word
"tyrannos" for "monarch." Theseus cor-
rects him at once. "There is no 'tyrannos'
here. This is a free city; and when I say a
free city, I mean one in which the whole
people by turns takes part in the sovereignty,
and the rich have no privilege as against the
poor" (399–408). These dissertations on
democratic government could stir men's passions and force their way into scenes of high
poetry legitimately enough at a time when
men were fighting and dying for their democracy. To those who are not "Lovers" of
the beautiful city they will seem cold and
irrelevant.

Other plays of this period show marks of
the same great wave of love for Athens. The

lost plays *Aigeus, Theseus, Erechtheus,* all on
Attic subjects, can be dated in the first years
of the war; the *Hippolytus* is built on an old
legend of the Acropolis and a poetic love of
Athens shines through the story. The *Andromache* especially is a curious document, the
meaning of which is discussed later on (p.
110). But the two plays we have described
at length, *The Children of Heracles* and the
Suppliant Women, give the best idea of what
patriotism meant to our poet. With most
men patriotism is a matter of association and
custom. They stick to their country because
it is theirs; to their own habits and prejudices
and even neighbours for the same reason.
But with Euripides his ideals came before his
actual surroundings. He loved Athens because Athens meant certain things, and if the
real Athens should cease to mean those things
he would cast her out of his heart. At least
he would try to do so; in point of fact that is
always a very difficult thing to do. But if
ever Athens should be false, it was pretty
certain that Euripides would find hatred
mingling with his betrayed love. There were
signs of this even in the *Medea* and the
Hecuba.

But before dealing with that subject we
must dwell for a few moments upon another

fine play, which marks in more than one sense the end of a period. The *Heracles*, written about the year 423, shows Theseus in the same rôle of Athenian hero. In the *Suppliant Women* he had helped Adrastus and the Argive mothers and shown them the path of true Hellenism; in the *Heracles* he comes to the rescue of Heracles in his fall. That hero has been mad and slain his own children; he has recovered and awakes to find himself bound to a pillar, with dead bodies that he cannot recognize round about him. He rages to be set free. He compels those who know to tell him the whole truth. Frantic with shame and horror, he wishes to curse God and die, when he sees Theseus approaching. Theseus has been his friend in many hard days and Heracles dares not face him nor speak to him. The touch of one so blood-guilty, the sound of his voice, the sight of his face, would bring pollution. He shrouds himself in his mantle and silently waves Theseus away. In a moment his friend's arms are round him, and the shrouding mantle is drawn off. There is no such thing as pollution; no deed of man can stain the immortal sunlight, and a friend's love does not fear the infection of blood. Heracles is touched: he thanks Theseus and is now ready to die. God has tempted him too far, and he will defy God. Theseus reminds him of what he is: the helper of man, the powerful friend of the oppressed; the Heracles who dared all and endured all; and now, like a common, weak-hearted man, he speaks of suicide! "Hellas will not suffer you to die in your blindness!" (1254). The great adventurer is softened and won over by the "wisdom" of Theseus, and goes to Athens to fulfil, in spite of suffering, whatever further tasks life may have in store for him.

This condemnation of suicide was unusual in antiquity; and the *Heracles* also contains one remarkable denial of the current myths, the more remarkable because, as Dr. Verrall has pointed out, it seems almost to upset the plot of the play. Heracles' madness is sent upon him by the malignity of Hera; we see her supernatural emissary entering the room where Heracles lies. And the hero himself speaks of his supernatural adventures. Yet he also utters the lines:

"Say not there be adulterers in Heaven
Nor prisoner gods and gaoler. Long ago
My heart has known it false and will not alter.
God, if he be God, lacketh naught. All these
Are dead unhappy tales of minstrelsy."
(*Her.* 1341; cf. *Iph. Taur.* 880-892; *Bellerophon* fr. 292.)

But in another way, too, the *Heracles* marks an epoch in the poet's life. It seems to have been written in or about the year 423, and it was in 424 that Euripides had reached the age of sixty and was set free from military service. He had had forty years of it, steady work for the most part; fighting against Boeotians, Spartans, Corinthians, against Thracian barbarians, in all probability also against other people further overseas. We have no record of the campaigns in which Euripides served; but we have by chance an inscription of the year 458, when he was twenty-six, giving the names of the members of one particular tribe, the Sons of Erechtheus, who fell in war in that one year. They had fallen "in Cyprus, in Egypt, in Phoenicia, at Halieis, in Aegina and at Megara." There were ten such tribes in Athens. And this record gives some notion of the extraordinary energy and ubiquity of the Athenian armies.

It is strange to reflect on the gulf that lies between the life of an ancient poet and his modern descendants. Our poets and men of letters mostly live either by writing or by investments eked out by writing. They are professional writers and readers and, as a rule, nothing else. It is comparatively rare

for any one of them to face daily dangers,
to stand against men who mean to kill him
and beside men for whom he is ready to die,
to be kept a couple of days fasting, or even
to work in the sweat of his body for the food
he eats. If such things happen by accident
to one of us we cherish them as priceless
"copy," or we even go out of our way to
compass the experience artificially.

But an ancient poet was living hard, working, thinking, fighting, suffering, through
most of the years that we are writing about
life. He took part in the political assembly,
in the Council, in the jury-courts; he worked
at his own farm or business; and every year
he was liable to be sent on long military ex-
peditions abroad or to be summoned at a
day's notice to defend the frontier at home.
It is out of a life like this, a life of crowded
reality and work, that Aeschylus and Sophocles and Euripides found leisure to write
their tragedies; one writing 90, one 127, and
the third 92! Euripides was considered in
antiquity a bookish poet. He had a library
—in numbers probably not one book for
every hundred that Tennyson or George
Meredith had: he was a philosopher, he read
to himself. But on what a background of
personal experience his philosophy was

builded! It is probably this immersion in the hard realities of life that gives ancient Greek literature some of its special characteristic. Its firm hold on sanity and common sense, for instance; its avoidance of sentimentality and paradox and various seductive kinds of folly; perhaps also its steady devotion to ideal forms and high conventions, and its aversion from anything that we should call "realism." A man everlastingly wrapped round in good books and safe living cries out for something harsh and real—for blood and swear-words and crude jagged sentences. A man who escapes with eagerness from a life of war and dirt and brutality and hardship to dwell just a short time among the Muses, naturally likes the Muses to be their very selves and not remind him of the mud he has just washed off. Euripides has two long descriptions of a battle, one in the *Children of Heracles* and one in the *Suppliant Women;* both are rhetorical Messenger's Speeches, conventionally well-written and without one touch that suggests personal experience. It is curious to compare these, the writings of the poet who had fought in scores of hand-to-hand battles, with the far more vivid rhapsodies of modern writers who have never so

much as seen a man pointing a gun at them.
Aeschylus indeed has written one splendid
battle piece in the *Persians*. But even
there there is no realism; it is the spirit of
the war of liberation that thrills in us as we
read, it is not the particular incidents of the
battle.

Forty years of military service finished:
as the men of sixty stepped out of the ranks
they must have had a feeling of mixed relief
and misgiving. They are now officially
"Gerontes," Old Men: they are off hard
work, and to be at the end of hard work is
perilously near being at the end of life.
There is in the *Heracles* a wistful chorus, put
in the mouths of certain Theban elders
(637 ff.), "Youth is what I love for ever; Old
Age is a burden upon the head, a dimness of
light in the eyes, heavier than the crags of
Etna. Fame and the crown of the East and
chambers piled with gold, what are they all
compared with Youth?" A second life is
what one longs for. To have it all again and
live it fully; if a man has any *aretê* in him,
any real life left in his heart, that is what
ought to be possible. . . . For Euripides
himself it seems there is still a life to be
lived. The words are important and almost
untranslatable. "I will never cease min-

gling together the Graces and the Muses"—
such words are nearly nonsense, like most
literal translations. The "Graces" or Char-
ities are the spirits of fulfilled desire, the
Muses are all the spirits of "Music" or of
"Wisdom"—of History and Mathematics,
by the way, just as much as Singing and
Poetry. "I will not rest. I will make the
spirits of Fulfilled Desire one with the
spirits of Music, a marriage of blessedness.
I care not to live if the Muses leave me;
their garlands shall be about me for ever.
Even yet the age-worn minstrel can turn
Memory into song."

Memory, according to Greek legend, was
the mother of the Muses; and the "memory"
of which Euripides is thinking is that of the
race, the saga of history and tradition, more
than his own. The Muses taught him long
ago their mystic dance, and he will be theirs
for ever; he will never from weariness or
faint heart ask them to rest. He was thinking doubtless of the lines of the old poet
Alcman to his dancing maidens, lines almost
the most beautiful ever sung by Greek lips:
"No more, ye maidens honey-throated,
voices of longing; my limbs will bear me no
more. Would God I were a ceryl-bird, over
the flower of the wave with the halcyons

flying, and never a care in his heart, the sea-
blue bird of the spring!" Euripides asks for
no rest: cares and all, he accepts the service
of the Muses and prays that he may bear
their harness to the end. It was a bold
prayer, and the Muses in granting it granted
it at a heavy price.

CHAPTER V

OUR Greek historians, with Thucydides at
their head, are practically unanimous in
associating with the Peloponnesian War a
progressive degradation and embitterment in
Greek public life, and a reaction against
the old dreams and ideals. We can measure
the change by many slight but significant
utterances.

When Herodotus records his opinion that
in the Persian Wars the Athenians had been
"the Saviours of Hellas" he has to preface
the remark by a curious apology (VII. 139):
"Here I am compelled by necessity to express an opinion which will be offensive to
most of mankind, but I cannot refrain from
putting it in the way which I believe to be
true." He was writing at the beginning of
the Peloponnesian War, and by that time
Athens was not the Saviour but "the Tyrant

105

City." Her "allies" had from time to time
refused to serve or tried to secede from the
alliance; and one by one she had reduced
them to compulsory subjection. The
"League" had become confessedly an
"Empire."

Even Pericles, the great statesman of the
good time, who had sought and achieved so
many fine ends, had failed to build up a free
League based on a representative elected
body. The possibility of such a plan had
hardly yet been conceived in the world,
though a rudimentary system of inter-
national councils did in some places exist
between neighbouring villages; and Pericles
must not be personally blamed for an error,
however fatal, which no one living knew how
to avoid. But he realized at last in 430 B.C.
what Athens had come to (*Thuc.* II. 63):
"Do not imagine you are fighting about a
simple issue, the subjection or independence
of certain cities. You have an Empire to
lose, and a danger to face from those who
hate you for your empire. To resign it now
would be impossible—if at this crisis some
timid and inactive spirits are hankering
after Righteousness even at that price! For
by this time your empire has become a
Despotism (Tyrannis), a thing which it is

considered unjust to acquire, but which can never be safely surrendered."

The same thought is emphasized more brutally by Cleon (*Thuc*. III. 37):

"I have remarked again and again that a democracy cannot govern an empire, and never more clearly than now. . . . You do not realize that when you make a concession to the allies out of pity, or are led away by their specious pleading, you commit a weakness dangerous to yourselves without receiving any gratitude from them. Remember that your empire is a Despotism exercised over unwilling men who are always in conspiracy against you." "Do not be misled," he adds a little later, "by the three most deadly enemies of empire, pity and charm of words and the generosity of strength" (*Thuc*. III. 40).

So much for the ideals of chivalry and freedom and "Sophia": for I think the second of Cleon's "enemies" refers especially to the eloquent wisdom of the philosophers. And as for democracy we do not hear now that "the very name of it is beautiful": we hear that it is no principle on which to govern an empire. And later on we shall hear Alcibiades, an Athenian of democratic antecedents, saying at Sparta:

"Of course all sensible men know what democracy is, and I better than most, from personal experience; but there is nothing new to be said about acknowledged insanity" (*Thuc.* **VI.** 89).

The ideals failed, and, if we are to believe our contemporary authors, the men failed too. Pericles, with all his errors, was a man of noble mind; he was pure in motive, lofty, a born ruler; he led his people towards "beauty and wisdom," and he wished it to be written on his grave that no Athenian had put on mourning through his act. Cleon, they all tell us, was a bellowing demagogue; violent, not over honest, unscrupulous, blundering; only resolute to fight for the demos of Athens till he dropped and to keep the poor from starving at whatever cost of blackmailing the rich and flaying the allied cities. And when he—by good luck, as Thucydides considers—was killed in battle, he was succeeded by Hyperbolus, a caricature of himself—as a pun of the comic poets' puts it, a "Cleon in hyperbole." This picture has been subjected to just criticism in many details, but it represents on the whole the united voice of our ancient witnesses.

One character only shines out in this

period with a lurid light. Alcibiades, so far
as one can understand him at all from our
fragmentary and anecdotal records, must
have been something like a Lord Byron on
a grand scale, turned soldier and statesman
instead of poet. His disastrous end and his
betrayal of all political parties have probably
affected his reputation unfairly. Violent and
unprincipled as he certainly was, the peculiar
dissolute caddishness implied in the anecdotes
is probably a misrepresentation of the kind
that arises so easily against a man who has no
friends. It needs an effort to imagine what
he looked like before he was found out. Of
noble birth and a nephew of Pericles; famous
for his good looks and his distinguished, if
insolent, manners; a brilliant soldier, an ambitious and far-scheming politician; a pupil
of the philosophers and an especially intimate friend of Socrates, capable both of rising
to great ideas and of expounding them to
the multitude; he was hailed by a large party
as the destined saviour of Athens, and seems
for a time at least to have made the same
impression upon Euripides. Even in the
Suppliant Women, peace-play as it is, Euripides congratulates Athens on possessing in
Theseus "a general good and young," and
critics have connected the phrase with the

election of Alcibiades, at a very early age, to
be General in the year 420. More significant
perhaps is the curious case of the *Andromache*.   The ancient argument tells us
definitely that it was not produced in Athens.
And we find from another source that it was
produced by one Democrates or Timocrates.
Now Euripides had a friend called Timocrates, who was an Argive; so it looks as if
the play had been produced in Argos. This
would be astonishing but by no means inex-
plicable. It was an old Athenian policy to
check Sparta by organizing a philo-Athenian
league in the Peloponnese itself (*Ar. Knights*,
465 ff.). The nucleus was to consist in three
states, Argos, Elis and Mantinea, which had
been visited by Themistocles just after the
Persian wars and had set up democracies on
the Athenian model. It was Alcibiades who
eventually succeeded in organizing this league
in 420, and it seems likely that the *Andromache* was sent to Argos for production in
much the same spirit in which Pindar used
to send his Chorus of Dancers with a new
song to compliment some foreign king. The
play seems to contain a reference to the
Peloponnesian War (734), it indulges in
curiously direct denunciations of the Spartans (445 ff., 595 ff.), and the Spartan Mene-

laus is the villain of the piece—a more stagey
villain than Euripides in his better moments
would have permitted. We have also one
doubtful external record of our poet's temporary faith in Alcibiades. In the year 420
there fell an observance of the Olympian
Festival, the greatest of all the Pan-Hellenic
Games, which carried with it a religious truce.
Alcibiades succeeded in getting Sparta con-
victed of a violation of this truce, and consequently excluded from the Festival, which
was a marked blow at her prestige. Then,
entering himself as a competitor, he won
with his own horses a whole series of prizes,
including the first, in the four-horse chariot
competition. And Plutarch, in his *Life of
Alcibiades*, refers to a Victory Ode which was
written for him on this occasion, "as report
goes, by the poet Euripides" (ch. 11). This
revival of the Pindaric *Epinikion* for a personal victory would fit in with the known
character of Alcibiades; and it would be a
sharp example of the irony of history if
Euripides consented to write the Ode.

Euripides' delusion was natural and it was
short-lived. The *Suppliant Women* points
towards peace, and the true policy of Alcibiades was to make peace impossible. And
even apart from that the ideals of the two men

were antipathetic. The matter is summed
up in the *Frogs* of Aristophanes, produced
in 405, when the only question remaining
about Alcibiades was whether he was more
dangerous to the city as an honoured leader or
as an enemy and exile. The two great poets
of the Dead are asked for their advice on this
particular subject and their answers are
clear. Aeschylus says: "Submit to the
lion's whelp"; Euripides rejects him with
three scathing lines (*Frogs*, 1427 ff., cf.
1446 ff.). Long before the date of the *Frogs*
Alcibiades had probably grown to be in the
mind of Euripides the very type and symbol
of the evil times.

All Greece—we have the emphatic and
disinterested testimony of Thucydides for
the statement—was gradually corrupted and
embittered by the long war. Probably all
war, as it accustoms people more and more
to desperate needs and desperate expedients
for meeting them, and sets more and more
aside the common generosities and humani-
ties of life, tends to some degradation of
character. But this particular war was
specially harmful. For one thing it was a
struggle not simply between two foreign
powers, but between two principles, oligarchy
and democracy. In almost all the cities of

the Athenian alliance t██ ██ ██ large numbers of malcontent ri█ ██ were only too
ready, if chance o█ ██ ██ to overthrow the
constitution, mas█ ██ the mob, and revolt
to Sparta. In █ ██od many of the cities on
the other side ██here were masses of discon-
tented poor who had been touched by the
breath of democratic doctrines, and were
anxious for a chance to cut the throats of
the ruling Few. It was like the state of
things produced in many cities of Europe
by the French Revolution. A secret civil
strife lay in the background b█ ██ the open
war; and the open war itse█ ██ a long
protracted struggle for life or d██ ██ Probably the most high-minded man when en-
gaged in a death-grapple fights in much the
same way as the most low-minded. And
there can be no doubt that as the toils
of war closed tighter round Athens, and
she began to feel herself fighting, gasp
by gasp, for both her empire and her life,
the ideals of the Saviour of Hellas fell
away from her. She fought with every
weapon that came.

Such times called forth naturally the men
that suited them. The assembly cared less
to listen to decent and thoughtful people, not
to speak of philosophers. It was feeling

bitter and fierce and frightened and it liked
speakers who were feeling the same.   The
same fear that made it cruel made it also
superstitious.   On one occasion the whole
city went mad with alarm because of a prank
played on some ancient figures of Hermes.
On another a great army was lost because it
and its general were afraid to move during
an eclipse of the moon. So soon had Anaxagoras been forgotten.

Is this the result, one is inclined to ask, of
the great ideals of democracy and enlightenment? Of course the old Tory type of Greek
historian, like Mitford, revelled in an affirma-
tive answer.   But a more reflective view of
history suggests a different explanation. We
must distinguish carefully between the two
notions, Enlightenment and Democracy.
They happen to have gone together in two
or three of the greatest periods of human progress and we are apt to regard them as somehow necessarily allied.   But they are not.
Doubtless Democracy is itself an exalted conception and belongs naturally to the ideas of
the Enlightenment, just as does the belief in
Reason, in the free pursuit of knowledge, in
justice to the weak, the wish to be right rather
than to be victorious, or the hatred of violence
and superstition as such. But the trouble is

that, in a backward and untrained people, the victory of democracy may result in the defeat of the other exalted ideas. The Athenian democracy as conceived by Pericles, Euripides or Protagoras was a free people, highly civilized and pursuing "wisdom," free from superstition and oppression themselves and helping always to emancipate others. But the actual rustics and workmen who voted for Pericles had been only touched on the surface by the "wisdom" of the sophists. They liked him because he made them great and admired and proud of being Athenians. But one must suspect that, when they were back at their farms and the spell of Pericles' "wisdom" was removed, they practised again the silliest and cruelest old agricultural magic, were terrified by the old superstitions, beat their slaves and wives and hated the "strangers" a few miles off, just as their grandfathers had done in the old times. What seems to have happened at the end of the war-time is that, owing largely to the democratic enthusiasm of the sophistic movement in Athens, the common people is strongly in power; owing to the same movement its old taboos and rules of conduct are a little shaken and less able to stand against strong tempta-tion; but meantime the true moral lessons

of the enlightenment, the hardest of all lessons
for man to learn, have never worked into their
bones. Just as the French Revolution called
into power the brutal and superstitious peasant who was the product of the Old Régime
and could never rise to the ideas of the Revolution, so the Athenian enlightenment had
put into power the old unregenerate mass of
sentiment that had not been permeated by
the enlightenment. Cleon was no friend of
sophists, but their avowed enemy. And when
he told the Assembly in its difficulties simply
to double the tribute of the allies and sack
their towns if they did not pay; when he
urged the killing in cold blood of all the Mity-
lenean prisoners, he was preaching doctrines
that would probably have seemed natural
enough in the old days, before any sophists
had troubled men's minds with talk about
duties towards dirty foreigners. And the
people who followed his lead were the same
sort of people who would naturally be terrified
about the mutilation of a taboo image or an
eclipse of the divine moon. What they had,
perhaps, acquired from the sophistic movement was a touch of effrontery. Boeotians
or Acarnanians might commit crimes, when
they needed to, by instinct, without stating
their reasons: in Athens you had at least to

discuss the principle of the proposed crime
and accept it for what it was worth. A
cynic or a hypocrite trained in a sophistic
school might offer occasional help with the
theory.

Perhaps the earliest touch of Euripides'
bitterness against his country comes, as we
have seen, in the *Hecuba* (p. 86). But the
period we have just reached, soon after the
Heracles, is marked by one of the most ironic
and enigmatical plays he ever wrote. The
Ion is interesting in every line and contains
one scene which is sometimes considered the
most poignant in all Greek tragedy, yet it
leaves every reader unsatisfied. Is it a pious
offering to Apollo, the ancestor of the Ionian
race? If so, why is Apollo the villain of the
piece? Is it a glorification of ancient Athens,
her legends and her shrines? If so, why are
the shrines polluted by lustful gods, the
legends made specially barbaric, and the
beautiful earth-born Princess shown as a se-
duced woman and a would-be murderess?
Nay, further, why does the hero of the play
explain in a careful speech that he would
sooner live a friendless slave in the temple at
Delphi than a free man and a prince in such
a place as Athens—a city "full of terror,"
where men "who are good and might show

wisdom are silent and never come forward,"
while the men in power watch enviously
round to destroy any possible rival? (598 ff.
Cf. Euripides' words in *Frogs*, 1446 ff.)   In
Delphi he has peace, and is not jostled off the
pavement by the scum of the earth (635)—a
complaint which is often made in Greek
literature about democratic Athens.

I think the best way to understand the *Ion*
is to suppose that Euripides, in his usual
manner, is just taking an old canonical legend,
seeing the human drama and romance in it,
and working it together in his own clear
ironic mind till at last he throws out his play,
saying: "There are your gods and your holy
legends;   see how you like them!"   The
irony is lurking at every corner, though
of course the drama and romance come
first.

The *Ion* is, of all the extant plays, the most
definitely blasphemous against the traditional gods.   Greek legend was full of stories
of heroes born of the love of a god and a
mortal woman.   Such stories could be turned
into high religious mysteries, as by Aeschylus
in his *Suppliant Women;* into tender and
reverent legends, as by Pindar in one or two
odes.   Euripides uses no such idealization.
In play after play, *Auge, Melanippe, Danae*,

Alope he seems to have scarified such gods,
as he does now in the *Ion*. Legend told that
Ion, the hero-ancestor of the Ionians, was
the son of the Athenian princess Creusa.
Creusa was married to one Xuthus, an Aeo-
lian soldier, but the real father of Ion was
the god Apollo. Euripides treats the story
as if Apollo were just a lawless ravisher,
utterly selfish and ready to lie when pressed,
though good-natured in his way when he
lost nothing by it—a sort of Alcibiades, in
fact. Xuthus is a butt; a foreigner with
abrupt and violent manners, lied to by
Apollo, befooled by his wife, disobeyed by
her maids, and eventually made happy by
the belief that her illegitimate son is really
his own. Creusa herself, though drawn with
extraordinary sympathy and beauty, is at
heart a savage.

Creusa, when she bore her child, laid him,
in her terror, in the same cavern where
Apollo had ravished her: surely the god
would save his own son. She came again
and the child was gone. As a matter of fact
the god had carried him in his cradle to
Delphi, where he was discovered by the
priestess and reared as a foundling in the
temple courts. Creusa was then married to
Xuthus, who knew nothing of her adven-

ture. Some seventeen years or so afterwards, since the pair had no children, they
came to Delphi to consult the god. Creusa
there meets the foundling, Ion, and the two
are strangely attracted to one another. She
almost confides to him her story, and he
tells her what he knows of his own. Meantime Xuthus goes in to ask the god for a
child; the god tells him that the first person
he meets on leaving the shrine will be his
son. (This, of course, is a lie.) He meets
Ion, salutes him as his son and embraces
him wildly. The boy protests: "Do not,"
cries Xuthus, "fly from what you should
love best on earth!" "I do not love teach-
ing manners to demented foreigners," retorts
the youth. Sobered by this, Xuthus tries,
with Ion's help, to think out what the god
can mean by saying that this youth is his
son. His married life has always been correct; but once when he was a young man,
there was a time . . . It was a great religious feast at Delphi and he was drunk.
Ion accepts the explanation, though he evidently does not much like his new father.
He makes difficulties about going to Athens.
He is sorry for Creusa. He wishes to stay as
he is. Xuthus decides that Creusa must be
deceived; he will say he has taken a fancy to

Ion and wishes to adopt him. Meantime let
them have a great birth-feast . . . and if
any of the Chorus say a word to Creusa they
shall be hanged! Creusa enters, accompanied by one of Euripides' characteristic
Old Slaves. The man has tended Creusa
from childhood, lives for her and thinks of
nothing else; he is utterly without scruple
apart from her. The Chorus immediately
tell Creusa what they know of the story.
Ion is Xuthus's illegitimate son; he must
have known it all the time; he has now, with
the god's connivance, arranged to take the
son back to Athens; as for Creusa, the god
says she shall have no child. Stung to fury
to think that her child is dead, that the boy
whom she so loved is deliberately deceiving
her, and that Apollo is adding this deliberate
insult to his old brutal wrong, Creusa casts
away shame and standing up in front of the
great Temple cries out her reproach against
the god. She is disgraced publicly and for
ever, but at least she will drag down this
devil who sits crowned and singing to the
lyre while the women he has ravished go mad
with grief and his babes are torn by wild
beasts. In the horror-stricken silence that
follows there is none to advise Creusa except
the old Slave. Blindly devoted and foster-

ing all her passions, he wrings from her line
by line the detailed story of her seduction,
and then calls for revenge. "Burn down the
god's temple!" She dare not. "Poison
Xuthus!" No; he was good to her when
she was miserable. "Kill the bastard!" . . .
Yes: she will do that. . . . The Slave takes
poison with him and goes to poison Ion at
the birth-feast. The plot fails; the Slave is
taken and Creusa, pursued by the angry
youth, flies to the altar. It is fury against
fury, each bewildered to find such evil in the
other, after their curious mutual attraction.
Here the Delphian Prophetess enters, bringing with her the tokens that were with the
foundling when she first came upon him in
the temple courts. Creusa, amazed, recognizes the old basket-cradle in which she had
exposed her own child.

She leaves the altar and gives herself up to
Ion. For a moment it seems as if he would
kill her; but he tests her story. What else
is there in the basket? She names the things,
her own shawl with gorgons on it, her own
snake-twined necklace and wreath of undy-
ing olive. The mother confesses to the son
and the son forgives her. But Apollo? What
of him? He has lied. . . . Ion, temple-
child as he is, is roused to rebellion: he will

break through the screen of the sanctuary
and demand of the god one plain answer—
when he is stopped by a vision of Athena.
She comes instead of Apollo, who fears to
face the mortals he has wronged; she bids
them be content and seek no further. Creusa
forgives the god; Ion remains moodily
silent.

The *Ion* is so rich in romantic invention
that it sometimes seems to a modern reader
curiously old-fashioned; it is full of motives
—lost children, and strawberry-marks, and
the cry of the mother's heart, and obvious
double meanings—which have been repeated
by so many plays since that we instinctively
regard them as "out of date." It is redeemed
by its passion and its sincere psychology. On
the other hand, it is more ironical than any
other extant Greek play. The irony touches
every part of the story, excepting the actual
tragedy of the wronged woman and the
charming carelessness of the foundling's life.
We should remember that an attack on the
god of Delphi was not particularly objectionable in Athens. For that god, by the
mouth of his official prophets, at the beginning of the war, had assured the Spartans
that if they fought well they would conquer
and that He, the God, would be fighting

for them. The best that a pious Athenian
could do for such a god as that was to suppose that the official prophets were liars.
Still Euripides attacks much more than
Delphi. If his thoughts ever strike home, it
is not merely Delphi that will fall, it is the
whole structure of Greek ritual and mythology. It is against the gods and against
Athens that his irony cuts sharpest.

Irony is the mood of one who has some
strong emotion within but will not quite
trust himself on the flood of it. And romance
is largely the mood of one turning away from
realities that disgust him. In the year 416
B.C. Euripides, in his relation to Athens,
was shaken for the first time out of any
thought of either romance or irony. During
the summer and winter of that year there
occurred an event of very small military
importance and no direct political conse-
quences, to which nevertheless Thucydides
devotes twenty-six continuous chapters in
a very significant part of his work, the part
just before the final catastrophe. The event
is the siege and capture by the Athenians of
a little island called Melos, the massacre
of all its adult men and the enslavement of
the women and children. The island had
no military power. It had little commerce

iian
sup-
liars.
than
ome, it
; is the
i myth-
against

ias some
iot quite
romance
way from
year 416
) Athens,
it of any
r. During
year there
ll military
ical conse-
Thucydides
chapters in
rk, the part
The event
Athenians of
he massacre
slavement of
e island had
:le commerce

and lived on its own poor agricul
population was not large: when i
populated five hundred colonists we
to people it again. Why then this l
in Thucydides' brief and severe i
Only, I think, because of the mora
volved and the naked clarity of t
Thucydides tells us of a long debat
the Athenian envoys and the Melia
and professes to report the argum
on each side. No doubt there is
artistic composition in the repc
cannot conclude that any Atheni
used exactly these horrible words.
can be sure that Thucydides tool
on Melos as the great typical exam
principles on which the Athenian
were led to act in the later part oi
we can go further and be almost
he selected it as a type of sin l
punishment—that sin of "Hubris'
which according to Greek ideas
ciated with some heaven-sent blin
pointed straight to a fall.

In cool and measured language
nian envoys explain to the Melian
for the populace is carefully exclu
it suits their purpose that Mel
become subject to their empire.

not pretend—being sensible men and talking to sensible men—that the Melians have
done them any wrong or that they have any
lawful claim to Melos, but they do not wish
any islands to remain independent: it is a
bad example to the others. The power of
Athens is practically irresistible: Melos is
free to submit or to be destroyed. The
Melians, in language carefully controlled
but vibrating with suppressed bitterness,
answer as best they can. Is it quite safe for
Athens to break all laws of right? Empires
are mortal; and the vengeance of mankind
upon such a tyranny as this . . . ? "We
take the risk of that," answer the Athenians;
"the immediate question is whether you
prefer to live or die." The Melians plead
to remain neutral; the plea is, of course,
refused. At any rate they will not submit.
They know Athens is vastly stronger in
men and ships and military skill; still the
gods may help the innocent ("That risk
causes us no uneasiness," say the envoys:
"we are quite as pious as you"); the Lace-
daemonians are bound by every tie of honour
and kinship to intervene ("We shall of course
see that they do not"); in any case we choose
to fight and hope rather than to accept
slavery. "A very regrettable misjudg-

ment," say the Athenians; and the war proceeds to its hideous end.

As I read this Melian Dialogue, as it is called, again and again, I feel more clearly the note of deep and angry satire. Probably the Athenian war-party would indignantly have repudiated the reasoning put into the mouths of their leaders. After all they were a democracy; and, as Thucydides fully recognizes, a great mass of men, if it does commit infamies, likes first to be drugged and stimulated with lies: it seldom, like the wicked man in Aristotle's Ethics, "calmly sins." [But in any case the massacre of Melos produced on the minds of men like Thucydides and Euripides —and we might probably add almost all the great writers who were anywise touched by the philosophic spirit—this peculiar impression. It seemed like a revelation of naked and triumphant sin.] And we can not but feel the intention with which Thucydides continues his story. "They put to death all the Melians whom they found of man's estate, and made slaves of the women and children. And they sent later five hundred colonists and took the land for their own.

"And the same winter the Athenians sought to sail with a greater fleet than ever before and conquer Sicily. . . ." This was

the great Sicilian expedition that brought
Athens to her doom.

Euripides must have been brooding on the
crime of Melos during the autumn and winter.
In the spring, when the great fleet was still
getting ready to sail, he produced a strange
play, the work rather of a prophet than a mere
artist, which was reckoned in antiquity as one
of his masterpieces but which set a flame of
discord for ever between himself and his
people. One would like to know what Archon
accepted that play and what rich man gave
the chorus. It was called *The Trojan Women*,
and it tells of the proudest conquest wrought
by Greek arms in legend, the taking of Troy
by the armies of Agamemnon. But it tells
the old legend in a peculiar way. Slowly, re-
flectively, with little stir of the blood, we are
made to look at the great glory, until we see
not glory at all but shame and blindness and
a world swallowed up in night. At the very
beginning we see gods brooding over the
wreck of Troy; as they might be brooding
over that wrecked island in the Aegean, whose
walls were almost as ancient as Troy's own.
It is from the Aegean that Poseidon has
risen to look upon the city that is now a smok-
ing ruin, sacked by the Greeks. "The shrines

are empty and the sanctuaries
blood." The unburied corpses
the air; and the conquering so
sick and uneasy, they know no
to and fro waiting for a wind t
them away from the country the
horrible. Such is the handiwor
daughter of Zeus! (46).

The name gives one a mome
Athena is so confessedly the tut
of Athens. But Euripides was o
the regular Homeric story, in v
had been the great enemy of 1
unscrupulous friend of the G
name is no sooner mentioned
pears. But she is changed. H
have gone too far; they hav
"Hubris," insulted the altars of
defiled virgins in holy places. A
is now turned against her pe
great fleet, flushed with conques
with sin, is just about to set
has asked Zeus the Father fo
against it, and Zeus has giver
hand. She and Poseidon swear
storm shall break as soon as
sail, and the hungry rocks of
be glutted with wrecked ship
men (95 ff.).

brought

ooding on the
nn and winter.
fleet was still
duced a strange
phet than a mere
a antiquity as one
ich set a flame of
himself and his
know what Archon
hat rich man gave
The Trojan Women,
st conquest wrought
, the taking of Troy
emnon. But it tells
liar way. Slowly, re-
ir of the blood, we are
eat glory, until we see
ame and blindness and
) in night. At the very
ods brooding over the
they might be brooding
and in the Aegean, whose
is ancient as Troy's own.
gean that Poseidon has
he city that is now a smok-
the Greeks. "The shrines

How are ye blind,
Ye treaders down of Cities; ye that cast
Temples to desolation and lay waste
Tombs, the untrodden sanctuaries where lie
The ancient dead, yourselves so soon to die!

And the angry presences vanish into the
night. Were the consciences of the sackers of
Melos quite easy during that prologue?

Then the day dawns and the play begins,
and we see what, in plain words, the great
glory has amounted to. We see the shattered
walls and some poor temporary huts where
once was a city; and presently we see a
human figure rising wearily from sleep. It is
an old woman, very tired, her head and her
back aching from the night on the hard
ground. The old woman is Hecuba, lately the
queen of Troy, and in the huts hard by are
other captives, "High women chosen from
the waste of war" to be slaves to the Greek
chieftains. They are to be allotted this morning. She calls them and they come startled
out of sleep, some terrified, some quiet, some
still dreaming, one suddenly frantic. Through
the rest of the play we hear bit by bit the
decisions of the Greek army-council. Cassandra, the virgin priestess, is to be Agamemnon's concubine. The stupid and good-
natured Herald who brings the news thinks

it good news. How lucky for the poor helpless girl! And the King, too! There is no
accounting for tastes; but he thinks it was
that air of unearthly holiness in Cassandra
which made Agamemnon fancy her. The
other women are horror-stricken, but Cassandra is happy. God is leading her; her
flesh seems no longer to be part of her; she
has seen something of the mind of God and
knows that the fate of Troy and of dead
Hector is better than that of their conquerors.
She sees in the end that she must discrown
herself, take off the bands of the priestess and
accept her desecration; she sees to what end
she is fated to lead Agamemnon, sees the
vision of his murdered body—murdered by
his wife—cast out in precipitous places on a
night of storm; and beside him on the wet
rocks there is some one else, dead, outcast,
naked . . . who is it? She sees it is herself, and goes forth to what is appointed
(445 ff.).

The central portion of the play deals with
the decision of the Greeks about Hector's
little boy, Astyanax. He is only a child now;
but of course he will grow, and he will form
the natural rallying point for all the fugitive
Trojans and the remnants of the great Trojan
Alliance. On the principles of the Melian

dialogue he is best out of the way. The
Herald is sent to take the child from his
mother, Andromache, and throw him over the
battlements. He comes when the two women, Andromache and Hecuba, are talking
together and the child playing somewhere
near. Andromache has been allotted as slave
to Pyrrhus, the son of Achilles, and is con-
sulting with Hecuba about the horror she has
to face. Shall she simply resist to the end, in
the hope that Pyrrhus may hate and kill her,
or shall she try, as she always has tried, to
make the best of things? Hecuba advises:
"Think of the boy and think of your own
gentle nature. You are made to love and not
to hate; when things were happy you made
them happier; when they are miserable you
will tend to heal them and make them less
sore. You may even win Pyrrhus to be kind
to your child, Hector's child; and he may
grow to be a help to all who have once loved
us. . . ." As they speak the shadow of the
entering Herald falls across them; he cannot
speak at first, but he has come to take the
child to its death, and his message has to be
given. This scene, with the parting between
Andromache and the child which follows,
seems to me perhaps the most absolutely
heart-rending in all the tragic literature of

the world.   After rising from it one under-
stands Aristotle's judgment of Euripides as
"the most tragic of the poets."

For sheer beauty of writing, for a kind of
gorgeous dignity that at times reminds one
of Aeschylus and yet is compatible with the
subtlest clashes of mood and character, the
Trojan Women stands perhaps first among all
the works of Euripides.   But that is not its
most remarkable quality.   The action works
up first to a great empty scene where the
child's body is brought back to his grand-
mother, Hecuba, for the funeral rites.   A solitary old woman with a dead child in her
arms;   that, on the human side, is the result
of these deeds of glory.   Then, in the finale,
come scenes of almost mystical tone, in
which Hecuba appeals first to the gods, who
care nothing;   then to the human dead who
did at least care and love;   but the dead, too,
are deaf like the gods and cannot help or heed.
Out of the noise and shame of battle there has
come Death the most Holy and taken them
to his peace.   No friend among the dead, no
help in God, no illusion anywhere, Hecuba
faces That Which Is and finds somewhere, in
the very intensity of Troy's affliction, a
splendour which cannot die.   She has reached
in some sense not the bottom, but the crown-

ing peak of her fortunes. Troy has already
been set on fire by the Greeks in preparation
for their departure, and the Queen rushes to
throw herself into the flames. She is hurled
back by the guards, and the women watch
the flaming city till with a crash the great
tower falls. The Greek trumpet sounds
through the darkness. It is the sign for the
women to start for their ships; and forth
they go, cheated of every palliative, cheated
even of death, to the new life of slavery. But
they have seen in their nakedness that there
is something in life which neither slavery nor
death can touch.

The play is a picture of the inner side of
a great conquest, a thing which then even
more than now, formed probably the very
heart of the dreams of the average unregenerate man. It is a thing that seemed beforehand to be a great joy, and is in reality a great
misery. It is conquest seen when the heat of
battle is over, and nothing remains but to
wait and think; conquest not embodied in
those who achieved it—we have but one
glimpse of the Greek conquerors, and that
shows a man contemptible and unhappy—but
in those who have experienced it most fully,
the conquered women.

We have so far treated the *Trojan Women*

as though it stood alone. In reality of course
it belonged to a group, and one cannot but
ask what the other plays were, and whether
their themes were such as could stand beside
this and not be shrivelled into commonplace
or triviality. Fortunately, though the plays
are both lost, we know something about
them. They were *Palamedes* and *Alexander;*
and both are on great subjects. The *Palamedes* tells of the righteous man condemned
by an evil world; the *Alexander* has for its
hero a slave.

Slavery had always been one of the subjects
that haunted Euripides. We do not happen
to find in our remains of his work any definite
pronouncement that slavery is "contrary to
nature," as was held by most Greek philosophers of the succeeding century. Probably
no practical man of the time could imagine
a large industrial city living without the in-
stitution of slavery. But it is clear that
Euripides hates it. It corrupts a man; it
makes the slave cowardly and untrust-
worthy. Yet "many slaves are better men
than their masters"; "many so-called free
men are slaves at heart." And again, in the
style of a Stoic, "A man without fear cannot
be a slave" (fr. 958: cf. fr. 86, 511, etc.).
Much more important than such statements

as these, which are, according to his manner, generally put in the mouth of a slave, are the many instances of "sympathetic" and courageous slaves, and the panegyrics on men who have no slaves but work with their own hands. These show the bent of the poet's mind. It is not, however, till the year of the *Trojan Women* that he takes the bold step of actually making a slave his hero and filling his play with discussions of slavery, including a definite contest in *areté* between the slaves and the masters. True, the slave turns out in the end to be a prince. The herdsman whose favourite bull the young nobles have seized for a sacrifice, and who pursues and challenges and eventually conquers them in strength and skill as well as magnanimity, turns out to be Alexander, son of Priam, who has been reared by the slave herdsmen of Mt. Ida. By our standards that is a pity. We should have preferred him a real slave. But probably on the Greek stage thus much of romance was inevitable, and after all it had its connection with real life. Many a Scythian and Thracian and even Phrygian chief, like this Alexander, must have stood for sale in Greek slave markets.

The root idea of the *Palamedes*, the righteous man falsely slain, has a momentous place

in the history of Greek thought. It starts, of
course, as a bitterness or a paradox. Righteousness to the fifth century Athenian was
almost identical with social service, and, in
a healthy society with normal conditions, the
man who serves his city well will naturally
be honoured by his city. But then comes the
thought, itself fraught with the wisdom of
the sophists: "What if the multitude is bent
on evil, or is blind? There are many men
who are evil but seem righteous; what if
the man who is righteous seems to be evil?"
Hence come the story of Aias in Pindar, and
Palamedes in this play, and the ideal Righteous Man of Plato's Republic who "shall be
scourged, tortured, bound . . . and at last
impaled or crucified" (*Rep.* p. 362a). The
idea runs through the various developments
of later Greek mysticism and attains its cul-
minating point in Christianity. It is in full
concord with the tone of the *Trojan Women.*

We know little of the *Palamedes.* That
hero was the true wise man, and his enemy
was Odysseus, the evil man who "seemed
wise" and had the ear of the multitude.
Palamedes is falsely accused of treason,
condemned by the unanimous voice of his
judges and sent to death. Fragments tell
us of some friend, perhaps a prisoner, carving

message after message upon oar-blades and
throwing them into the sea that the truth
might be known; and we have two beautiful untranslatable lines uttered by the
Chorus: "Ye have slain, ye Greeks, ye
have slain the nightingale; the wingéd-one
of the Muses who sought no man's pain."
Tradition saw in the words a reference to
the wise Protagoras, lately slandered to his
death.

The consideration of these other plays of
the same trilogy strengthens the impression
that I receive already from the *Trojan
Women*, an impression of some deepening of
experience, some profound change that has
worked into the writer's soul. Other critics,
and notably Wilamowitz and Mr. Glover,
have similarly felt that this play marks a
turning point. It was not a change of front;
it was not sudden; it was not dependent on
visions or supernatural messages. It was
the completion of a long process of strong
feeling and intense thought, not the less
sane because of its decided element of mysticism. It probably differed in many ways
from the sudden and conscious conversions
which began the ministry of certain Greek
philosophers, both Cynic and Stoic, in the
fourth and third centuries before Christ.

It differed still more from the experience of
Paul on the road to Damascus or Augustine
beneath the fig-tree. But it does seem to me
that in this tragedy the author shows a
greatly increased sense of some reality that
is behind appearances, some loyalty higher
than the claims of friends or country, which
supersedes as both false and inadequate the
current moral code and the current theologies.

CHAPTER VI

AFTER THE "TROJAN WOMEN": EURIPIDES' LAST YEARS IN ATHENS: FROM THE "IPHIGENIA" TO THE "ORESTES"

CRITICS have used various words to describe the change of mood which followed the *Trojan Women*. They speak of a period of despair, pessimism, progressive bitterness, *Verzweiflung und Weltschmerz*. But such phrases seem to me misleading. In the first place I do not think they describe quite truly even the particular plays they are meant to describe; in the second, they do not allow for the great variety which subsists in the plays of this period. The mood of the *Trojan Women* is not exactly pessimism or despair; and whatever it is, it does not colour all the subsequent plays.

The plays after 415 fall into two main divisions. First the works of pure fancy or romance, in which the poet seems to turn intentionally away from reality. Such are the *Iphigenia in Tauris*, the *Helena* and the *Andromeda;* they move among far seas and

140

strange adventures and they have happy
endings. Next there are the true tragedies,
close to life, ruthlessly probing the depths
of human nature; not more acutely bitter
than such earlier works as the *Medea* and
Hecuba, but with a bitterness more profound
because it is comparatively free from indignation. The glory has fallen away and
the burning anger with it. The poor miserable heroes and heroines . . . what else can
you expect of them? Rage is no good; punishment worse than useless. The road to
healing lies elsewhere.

A good key to the first of these types of
play is to be seen in Aristophanes' comedy,
The Birds. The gayest, sweetest and most
irresponsible of all his plays, it was written
just after the news of the final disaster in
Sicily, when ruin stared Athens in the face.
And the two heroes of it, disgusted with the
ways of man, depart to live among the birds
and build, with their help, a splendid Cloud
City. In much the same spirit Euripides
must have written his *Andromeda.* He produced it in 412, the same year in which he
was invited by the anti-war government
which came into power after the news of the
great disaster to write the national epitaph
on the soldiers slain in Sicily. He wrote the

epitaph in the old severe untranslatable
style of Simonides: "These men won eight
victories over the Syracusans when the hand
of God lay even between both." In English
it seems cold; it seems hardly poetry. But
in Greek it is like carved marble. Then,
one must imagine, he turned right away
from the present and spent his days with
Andromeda. Only a few fragments of the
Andromeda remain, but they are curiously
beautiful; and the play as a whole seems to
have been the one unclouded love-romance
that Euripides ever wrote. It was fantastic,
remote from life, with its heroine chained to
a cliff over the blue sea awaiting the approach
of the sea-monster, and its hero, Perseus, on
winged sandals, appearing through the air
to save her. Yet the fragments have a wistful ring: "O holy Night, how long is the path
of thy chariot!" "By the Mercy that
dwelleth in the sea caves, cease, O Echo;
let me weep my fill in peace." Or the
strange lines (fr. 135):

> Methinks it is the morrow, day by day,
> That cows us, and the coming thing alway
> Greater than things to-day or yesterday.

There was a story told, in later times, of a
tragedy-fever that fell on the folk of Abdèra,

in Thrace, through this play, till in every
street you could see young men walking as
though in a dream, and murmuring to themselves the speech beginning, "O Love, high
monarch over gods and men. . . ." The
Andromeda was five hundred years old when
people told that story.

The *Iphigenia in Tauris* came one year
earlier. It is one of the most beautiful of the
extant plays, not really a tragedy in our
sense nor yet merely a romance. It begins
in gloom and rises to a sense of peril, to
swift and dangerous adventure, to joyful
escape. So far it is like romance. But it is
tragic in the sincerity of the character-
drawing. Iphigenia, especially, with her
mixed longings for revenge and for affection,
her hatred of the Greece that wronged her
and her love of the Greece that is her only
home, her possibilities of stony cruelty and
her realities of swift self-sacrifice, is a true
child of her great and accursed house. The
plot is as follows:—Iphigenia, daughter of
Agamemnon, who was supposed to have
been sacrificed by her father at Aulis, was
really saved by Artemis and is now priestess
to that goddess in the land of the Taurians
at the extremity of the Friendless Sea. The
Taurians are savages who kill all strangers,

and if ever a Greek shall land in the wild
place it will be her task to prepare him for
sacrifice. She lives with this terror hanging
over her, and the first Greek that comes is
her unknown brother, Orestes. Their recognition of one another is, perhaps, the
finest recognition-scene in all Tragedy; and
with its sequels of stratagem and escape
forms a thrilling play, haunted not, like a
tragedy, by the shadow of death but rather
by the shadow of homesickness. The characters are Greeks in a far barbarian land,
longing for home or even for the Greek sea.
The lyrics are particularly fine, and most
of them full of sea-light and the clash of
waters.

In the same year as the *Andromeda* came
another romantic play, the *Helena*. It is a
good deal like the *Iphigenia* in structure, but
it is lighter, harder, and more artificial. The
romance of Euripides is never quite the easy
dreaming of lighter-hearted writers. And
the *Helena*, in which he seems to have attempted a work of mere fancy, is, if we understand it rightly, a rather brilliant failure.
Some critics—quite mistakenly in my judgment—have even argued that it is a parody.
The plot is based on a variant of the canonical legend about Helen, a variant generally

associated with the ancient lyric poet, Stesichorus. Story tells that Stesichorus at one time lost his eyesight and took it into his head that this was a punishment laid on him by the goddess Helen, because he had told the story of her flight with Paris from her husband's house. He wrote a recanta-*Palinode* tion, based on another form of the Helen-legend, in which Helen was borne away by the God Hermes to Egypt and there lived like a true wife till Menelaus came and found her. The being that went with Paris to Troy was only a phantom image of Helen, contrived by the gods in order to bring about the war, and so reduce the wickedness and multitude of mankind. In Euripides' play *Mozart's* there is a wicked king of Egypt, who seeks *Zauberflöte* to marry Helen against her will and kills all Greeks who land in his country. The war at Troy is over, and Menelaus, beaten by storms out of his way, is shipwrecked on the coast of Egypt. He and Helen meet, recognize one another, and by the help of the king's sister, who has second sight, contrive to escape. It is hard to say what exactly is wrong with the *Helena;* and it may only be that we moderns do not know in what spirit to take it. But the illusion is difficult to keep up and the work seems cold. Reality has gone out of it. For one thing, Helen, in her thorough process of rehabilitation, has emerged that most in-sipid of fancies, a perfectly beautiful and blameless heroine with no character except love of her husband, whom, by the way, she has not seen for seventeen years.

Another large experiment of this time is the *Phoenissae*, or *Tyrian Women* (410?). It is the longest Greek tragedy in existence, and covers the greatest stretch of story. Aeschylus, we remember, had the habit of writing true "trilogies"—three continuous dramas, carrying on the same history. The *Phoenissae* seems like an attempt to run the matter of a whole trilogy into one play. It does not fall into either of the divisions which I have sketched above: it is neither a play of fancy nor yet a realistic tragedy. But even if we had no external tradition of its date we could tell to what part of the author's life it belongs. It is written, as it is conceived, in the large and heroic style; but it shows in the regular manner of this period a general clash of hatreds and frantic ambitions and revenges and cruel states-manship standing out against the light of a young man's heroism and a mother's and a sister's love. It is like Euripides, too, that this beautiful mother should be Jocasta,

whose unknowing incest had made her
an abomination in the eyes of orthodox
Greece.

The play tells the story of Thebes. The
sin of Oedipus and Jocasta is a thing of the
past; Oedipus has blinded himself and
cursed his children, and they have in course
of time imprisoned him in the vaults of the
palace. Jocasta still lives. The sons Polyneices and Eteocles have agreed to reign by
turns; Polyneices, the elder, has reigned his
year and gone abroad to Argos; Eteocles
having once got the crown has refused to
yield it up. Polyneices comes with an Argive army to lay siege to Thebes and win
his rights by war. The drama is developed
in a series of great pictures. We have first
the Princess Antigone with an old slave
looking from the wall out towards the
enemy's camp, seeking for a glimpse of her
brother. Next comes a man with face
hidden and sword drawn stealing through
the gates, seeking for Jocasta. It is Polyneices. The mother has induced her sons to
have one meeting before they fight. The
meeting reveals nothing but ambition and
mutual hatred. They agree to look for one
another on the field, and Polyneices goes.
There are consultations in the beleaguered

city. Creon, who is Jocasta's brother and a
sort of Prime Minister, advises the rash
Eteocles; but the prophets must be con-
sulted too, that the gods may be favorable.
The prophet Tiresias—blind and old and
jealous, as so often in Greek tragedy—proclaims that the only medicine to save the
state is for Creon's son, Menoikeus, to be
slain as a sin-offering in the lair of the ancient Dragon whom Cadmus slew. Creon
quickly refuses; he dismisses the prophet
and arranges for his son to escape from
Thebes and fly to the ends of Greece. The
boy feigns consent to the plan of escape, but,
as soon as his father has left him, rushes en-
thusiastically up to a tower of the city and
flings himself over into the Dragon's den.
A messenger comes to Jocasta with news of
the battle. "Are her sons slain?" No;
both are alive and unhurt. He tells his story
of the Argive attack and its repulse from
every gate.—"But what of the two brothers?"—He must go now and will bring more
news later.—Jocasta sees he is concealing
something and compels him to speak. The
truth comes out; the brothers are preparing a single combat. With a shriek the
mother calls Antigone; and the two women,
young and old, make their way through the

army to try to separate the blood-mad men. We learn from a second messenger how the brothers have slain each other "in a meadow of wild lotus," and Jocasta has killed herself with one of their swords. Antigone returns and to bring the news to her only friend, the blind Oedipus. Creon by Eteocles' charge takes over the government, he, too, a broken-hearted man, but none the less ruthless; he proclaims that Polyneices' body shall lie unburied and that Oedipus, the source of pollution, shall be cast out of the land; Antigone meantime shall marry Creon's son, Haemon. Antigone defies him. She will not wed Haemon nor any of Creon's kin: her father shall not be cast out to die, for she will go with him and protect him. Polyneices shall not lie unburied, for she herself will return by stealth and bury him. There is still one human love that Oedipus yearns for most; that of the sin-stained wife and mother who is lying dead in the meadow of wild lotus. But meantime he takes the hand of his daughter. Old man and young maiden they go forth together, away from the brutalities of human kind, to the high mountains, to the holy inviolate places on Kithairon where only the wild White Women of Dionysus dance their mystic dances.

The *Phoenissae* stands half way between
the pure Romances and the tragedies of the
last period. Of these latter the clearest type
is the *Electra* (probably 413), a play which
before it was understood used to receive the
unstinted abuse of Critics, as "the meanest
of Greek tragedies," "the very worst of all
Euripides' plays." It deals with the moral
problem of the Blood-Feud, stated in its
sharpest terms.

Now the blood-feud, we must realize, in
any society where there is no public law and
no police, is a high moral duty. A man commits an abominable crime and revels in comfort on the proceeds; his victim is dead, and
there is no law which will act automatically.
It becomes the duty of some one—normally
the heir or representative of the dead man
—to devote himself to the work of justice,
to forsake all business and pleasure in life till
the wrong has been righted and the dead man
avenged. A man who would let his kinsman
be murdered and then live on at his ease
rather than pursue the murderer, would
obviously be a poor false creature. Now
comes the problem. The strongest possible
claim is that of a father murdered; the most
horrible act a Greek could conceive was for a
man to slay his mother. Suppose a wife

murdered her husband, ought her son to slay
her? The law of the blood-feud, as tradi-
tionally preached from the Temple of Apollo
at Delphi, answered, in spite of all repug-
nances, Yes.

The story had been treated before Euripides by many poets, including Homer,
Stesichorus, Pindar, Aeschylus and possibly
—though the dates are not certain—Sophocles. Clytemnestra had with the help of her
lover Aegisthus murdered her husband Agamemnon; her son Orestes slays her in obedience to Apollo's command, and his sister
Electra aids him. Aeschylus in his *Libation-
Bearers* had dealt with this theme on broad
lines and with gorgeous intensity of imagination. His Orestes is carried to the deed on a
great wave of religious passion and goes mad
as soon as it is done. The deed as commanded
by God is right, but it is too much for human
nature to endure. In an ensuing play Orestes,
after long sufferings, is tried for the matricide
and, when the human judges are evenly
divided, acquitted by the divine voice of
Athena. Sophocles treats the subject very
differently. He makes a most brilliant play
with extraordinary clashes of emotion and
moments of tragic beauty. But, evidently of
set purpose, he makes the whole treatment

hard and archaic. There is no shrinking
back, no question of conscience at all. Clytemnestra is a furious tyrant; she beats
Electra with her fists, and Aegisthus does
worse (1196, 517). The climax of the play
is not the mother-murder but the killing of
Aegisthus, which was presumably the harder
and more exciting job. When Orestes and his
friend Pylades come out of the palace stream-
ing with Clytemnestra's blood their nerves
are unshaken and the Chorus is careful to say
that they are not to be in any way blamed
(1423).

The spirit of Euripides is exactly the opposite; so much so indeed that most critics
feel clear that the two *Electra* plays are closely
related, and related in opposition. The one
is a deliberate protest against the other;
unfortunately the play of Sophocles cannot
be dated and it is not clear from internal evidence which play was written first.

In the *Electra* of Euripides we find two
main qualities. First, there is psychological
realism of the subtlest kind. Secondly, there
is a new moral atmosphere. With a power of
sympathy and analysis unrivalled in ancient
drama he has imagined just what kind of
people these children must have been, who
would thus through long years nurse the seeds

of hatred and at the end kill their mother. He studies them all; Electra, a mixture of heroism and broken nerves; a poisoned and haunted woman, eating her heart in ceaseless broodings of hate and love, both alike unsatisfied; for he suggests, somewhat cruelly, that she might have lived contentedly enough, had she only had a normal married life. The name in its original Doric form suggested the meaning, "*Unmated*." Orestes is a youth bred in the unwholesome dreams of exile, and now swept away by his sister's stronger will; subject also, as Orestes always is in Greek tragedy, to delusions and melancholy madness. The mother herself is not forgotten, and a most piteous figure she shows, "this sad, middle-aged woman, whose first words are an apology; controlling quickly her old fires, anxious to be as little hated as possible; ready even to atone for her crime, if only there were some safe way of atonement." Thus, in the first place, Euripides has stripped the old bloody deed of the heroic glamour that surrounded it. His actors are not clear-minded heroes moving straight to their purpose. They are human creatures, erring, broken by passion, mastered by their own inhibitions and doubts and regrets. In the second place he has no doubt at all about the ethics of the mother-murder. It was an abomination, and the god who ordained it—if any did—was a power of darkness.

After the deed the two murderers come forth as in Sophocles. But this time they are not triumphant and the Chorus does not hail them as having done right. They reel from the door, "red-garmented and ghastly" and break into a long agony of remorse. The Chorus share their horror. Electra's guilt is the greater since she drove her brother to the deed against his will; even while they love her, they can not quite forget that, though they feel that now at last, by this anguish, her heart may be "made clean within." The play ends with an appearance of the gods. The Heavenly Horsemen, Castor and Polydeuces, who were kinsmen of the dead, appear on a cloud, and speak in judgment and comfort. With a definiteness rare in Euripides they pronounce the deed of vengeance to be evil:

> "And Phœbus, Phœbus . . . Nay:
> He is my lord, therefore I hold my peace.
> But though in light he dwell, not light was this
> He showed to thee, but darkness."

Another note is also struck, that of pity for the suffering of humanity. Orestes and

Electra, condemned to part, break, as they bid one another farewell, into a great cry, and the gods, hearing it, are shaken:

> Alas! what would ye? For that cry
>   Ourselves and all the sons of heaven
>   Have pity; yea, our peace is riven
> By the strange pain of these that die.
>
>   *   *   *   *   *
>
> But hark!   The far Sicilian sea
>   Calls, and a noise of men and ships
>   That labour sunken to the lips
> In bitter billows; forth go we
> With saving.

They speak such words of comfort and groping wisdom as they can find—no one has ever claimed that they are omniscient—and depart upon their own eternal task, which is not to punish but to save.

The appearance of the gods in the *Electra* is so beautiful that no critics have yet tried to explain it away as nonsense; and the lesson of it so clear that its meaning is seldom denied. But I find just the same lesson in the final scene of the *Orestes*, which is commonly taken as the very worst instance of Euripides' habit of closing with a "God from the machine."

The *Orestes* (408 B.C.) deals with the fate of Orestes some days after his mother's murder. He is mad and sick; his sister is nursing

him with devotion. The people have risen
against them and they are held prisoners in
the palace till an assembly shall try them for
murder and pronounce their fate. Meantime
Menelaus—Orestes' uncle and king of Sparta
—has arrived at the harbour with his wife
Helen and their daughter Hermione. He has
sent on his wife and daughter to the palace
and is expected hourly himself. He is
Agamemnon's brother; he has with him an
army of Trojan veterans; he can surely be
counted on to cow the Argive populace and
save his dead brother's son. All our hopes
hang on Menelaus, and when at last he comes
he proves false. He would like to help; but
it would be wrong for him, a foreigner, to
dictate to the Argives; and he has only a very
small force with him. However, he will
reason with Orestes' enemies. One does not
forget that, if Argos is left without a king,
Menelaus will normally inherit. The sick
man blazes into rage against him and Menelaus becomes an open enemy. Exasperation
follows on exasperation: Orestes' friend
Pylades breaks through the guards and enters
the palace to share the prisoners' fate. The
assembly hears and at length condemns them.
They are given a day in which to die as they
best please. Like scorpions surrounded by

fire, the three, Orestes, Electra and Pylades,
begin to strike blindly. A brilliant idea!
They can kill Helen: that will punish Menelaus, and Helen deserves many deaths. Better
still, kill Helen and then capture Hermione!
Hold a dagger at her throat and then bargain
with Menelaus for help even at the last hour!
Murder his wife and then force him to help!
Splendid! The madness of Orestes infects
the whole play. Helen escapes, being half-
divine; but they catch Hermione, who, as a
matter of fact, has always been kind to them.
Menelaus, who has heard news from an
escaping slave, rushes up to save Helen, but
he finds no sign of her; he finds only the palace
barred and the madman on the roof, shriek-
ing derision and holding the knife at his
daughter's throat. There is a brief wild attempt at bargaining; then hate in Menelaus
overcomes fear. He rejects all terms.
Orestes' party sets fire to the palace; and
Menelaus at the head of his soldiers beats
blindly at the barred gate. "The fire of Hell,"
to use Dr. Verrall's phrase, has been let
loose; rage, hatred, revenge, all blazing to
the point of madness; what more can
befall?

What does befall is strange and daring.
An entry of a god not in gentleness, not with

any preparation or introducton, but sudden and terrific, striking all beholders into a trance from which they awaken changed men. The point has not been generally observed, though it is, I think, clear.

At Apollo's first sudden cry "Menelaus, be still!" (line 1625) we know that Orestes is supporting Hermione in one arm while with the other hand he is holding the knife at her throat. He is in exactly the same position at line 1653; he only moves from it at 1671. That is the conduct of a man in a trance, suddenly, as it were, struck rigid. And we shall find that the words spoken by both Menelaus and Orestes when Apollo has finished his charge, are like nothing but the words of men emerging from a trance, a trance, too, of some supernatural kind, like that for instance which falls on the raging world in Mr. Wells's book, *In the Days of the Comet*. Here, too, a raging world wakes to find itself at peace and its past hatreds unintelligible. And the first thought that comes to the surface is, in each case, the great guiding preoccupation of each man's life; with Menelaus it is Helen; with Orestes the oracle that made him sin. Nay more; when Orestes wakens, half-conscious, to find Hermione lying in his arms, his natural movement, as experiments on hypnotized persons have shown, is to accept the suggestion and draw her to him in love. Greek legend knew well that, as a matter of history, Hermione became Orestes' bride. There is daring, perhaps excessive daring, in making it occur this way; but the psychology of something like hypnotism had a fascination for both Aeschylus and Euripides. For the rest, Apollo has spoken the word of forgiveness and reconciliation. He concludes:

> Depart now, each upon his destined way,
> Your hates dead and forgotten.

MEN.   I obey.

OR.   I too; mine heart is as a wine of peace
        Poured with the past and thy dark mysteries.

APOLLO   Go now your ways: and without cease
             Give honour in your hearts to one,
             Of spirits all beneath the sun
           Most beautiful; her name is Peace.

            I rise with Helen Zeus-ward, past
             The orb of many a shining star;
             Where Heracles and Hebe are
           And Hera, she shall reign at last,

            A goddess in men's prayers to be
             For ever, with her Brethren twain
             Enthronèd, a great help in pain
           And queen of the eternal sea.

"Helen a goddess!" say some critics; "the notion is impossible. We have seen her in

this same play, a heartless ordinary woman."
Yet I think Euripides was serious enough.
I do not say he believed either this or any
other particular bit of the mythology. But
he was writing seriously and aiming at
beauty, not at satire. 'All legend said that
Helen was made a goddess; and Euripides
was always curiously haunted by the thought
of Helen and by the mysterious and deadly
power of mere superlative beauty. As Apollo
had said to Menelaus (1638):

> Thy bride shall be another: none may know
> Her. For the Gods, to work much death and woe,
> Devised this loveliness all dreams above,
> That men in Greece and Troy for thirst thereof
> Should strive and die, and so the old Earth win
> Peace from mankind's great multitude and sin.

The superlative beauty may probably
enough be found in company with heartless-
ness and treachery; but cannot these things
be purged away, like the hates of Menelaus
and Orestes, and the pure beauty remain a
thing to pray to and be helped by, much as
the old sagas pretend? There is here again
the touch of mysticism.

But however it be about Helen, or even
about the above explanation in detail of the
last scene of the *Orestes*, it is clear that both
the most characteristic plays of the so-called

period of gloom end with a strong, almost a
mystically strong, note of peace and reconciliation.   This note occurs, though with
less intensity, at the end of other late plays,
such as the *Iphigenia in Tauris* and the
Helena; and, though without a god, in the
Phoenissae. It does not occur at all in the
early plays. The *Medea* and *Hecuba* end in
pure hate; the *Hippolytus* ends in wonderful beauty and a reconciliation between
the hero and his father, who are natural
friends, but it keeps up the feud of Aphrodite and Artemis and contains a strange
threat of vengeance (v. 1420 ff.).   The
lovely Thetis of the *Andromache* brings comfort and rest but preaches no forgiveness;
on the contrary the body of Pyrrhus is to be
buried at Delphi as an eternal reproach.
Euripides all through his life was occupied
with the study of revenge. It was a time,
as Thucydides tells us, when "men tried to
surpass all the record of previous times in
the ingenuity of their enterprises and the
enormity of their revenges."   Euripides
seems first to have been almost fascinated
by the enormous revenges, at least when
they were the work of people who had suffered enormous wrong. He seems, in plays
like the *Medea,* to be saying: "If you goad

people beyond endurance, this is the sort of thing you must expect them to do . . . and serve you right!" In the plays after 415 the emphasis has rather changed: "You must expect to be wronged, and revenge will do good to nobody. Seek peace and forgive one another."

CHAPTER VII

MACEDONIA: THE "IPHIGENIA IN AULIS"; THE "BACCHAE"

THUS we come round to the figure from which we started, the old sad man with the long beard, who,seldom laughed and was not easy to speak to; who sat for long hours in his seaward cave on Salamis, meditating and perhaps writing one could not tell what, except indeed that it was "something great and high." It was natural that he should be sad. His dreams were overthrown; his City, his Beloved, had turned worse than false. Public life was in every way tenfold more intimate and important to an ancient Greek than it is to us moderns who seldom eat a muttonchop the less when our worst political enemies pass their most detested bills. And Athens had not only been false to her ideals; she had sinned for the sake of success and had then failed. And her failure probably made the daily life of her citizens a thing of anxiety and discomfort. You

163

were never quite sure of your daily food.
You were never quite safe from a triumphant
raid of the enemy. And the habitual bodily
discomfort which is the central fact of old
age must have had for Euripides much to
aggravate and little to soften it.

It was natural, too, that his people should
hate him. Nations at war do not easily
forgive those who denounce their wars as
unjust; when the war, in spite of all heroism,
goes against them, their resentment is all
the bitterer. There is, of course, not the
ghost of a suggestion in Euripides that he
thought the Spartans right or that he wished
Athens to be defeated; far from it. But the
Athenian public was not in a mood for subtle
distinctions, and his air of disapproval was
enough. Besides, thought the meaner among
them, the man was a known blasphemer.
He had been the friend of the sophists; he
had denied the gods; worse, he had denounced the doings of the gods as evil.
These misfortunes that hurtled round the
City's head must surely be sent for some
good reason. Very likely just because the
City, corrupted by the "charm of words,"
had allowed such wicked sophists to live.
He was at one time prosecuted for impiety;
we do not know the date or the details, but

he seems to have been acquitted. The day
of Socrates had not yet come. But other
charges remained. He was a wicked old
man: he had preached dreadful things
about women; he had defended in his plays
adulteresses and perjurers and workers of
incest. What must his personal life be, if
these were his principles? No wonder that
he lived so secretly, he and his wife and that
dark-skinned secretary, Cephisophon!

Perhaps he was a miser and had secret
stores of wealth? We hear of an action
brought against him on these lines. A certain Hygiainon was selected, as a rich man,
to perform some "Liturgy" or public service at his own cost, and he claimed that
Euripides was richer and should be made to
do it instead. We do not know the result
of the trial; we only know that the plaintiff
attempted to create prejudice against Euripides by quoting the line of the *Hippolytus*
(see above p. 86) which was supposed to
defend perjury.

These things were annoyances enough.
But there must have been some darker cloud
that fell over Euripides' life at this time.
For we are not only told in the Lives that
"The Athenians bore a grudge against him,"
and that "he lost patience with the ill-will

of his fellow-citizens," but one of our earliest
witnesses, Philodemus, says that when he
left Athens he did so "in grief, because
almost all in Athens were rejoicing over him."
The word used means, like the German
"Schadenfreude," rejoicing at another's injury. So there must have been some injury
for them to rejoice at.

The old Satyrus tradition, with its tone
of scandal and misunderstanding, says that
his wife was false to him, but the story will
not bear historical criticism. And it would
not be safe to use so rotten a foundation to
build any theory upon, however likely it
may be in itself that a man of this kind
should meet with domestic unhappiness in
one or other of its many forms. In thinking
of Euripides one is constantly reminded of
Tolstoy. And there are many ways of making husbands miserable besides merely be-
traying them.

Whatever the cause, shortly after the
production of the *Orestes* in 408 the old
poet's endurance snapped, and, at the age
apparently of seventy-six, he struck off into
voluntary exile. It is only one instance
among many of his extraordinary vital force.
The language of the ancient Life is unfortunately confused just here, but it seems to

say that he went first to Magnesia, with
which city he had had relations in earlier
days. He had been granted some civic
honours there, and had acted as Proxenus
—a kind of consul or general protector—for
Magnesians in Athens. There was more
than one town of the name. But the one
meant is probably a large town in the
Maeander Valley, not far from Ephesus. It
lay in Persian territory, but had been granted
by Artaxerxes to the great Themistocles as
a gift, and was still ruled, subject to the
Persian king, by Themistocles' descendants.
Doubtless it was to them that the poet
went. We know nothing more, except that
he did not stay long in Magnesia, but went
on to another place where barbarians or
semi-barbarians were ruled by a Greek
dynasty.

The king of Macedon, Archelaus, an able
despot who was now laying the seeds of the
great kingdom which, before the lapse of a
century, was to produce Philip and Alexander the Great, had always an eye for men
of genius who might be attracted to his
court. He had invited Euripides before
and now renewed his invitation. Other men
of "wisdom" were already with Archelaus.
Agathon, the tragic poet; Timotheus, the

now famous musician whom Euripides had
once saved, so the story ran, from suicide;
Zeuxis, the greatest painter of the time; and
perhaps also Thucydides, the historian.   It
would not be like living among barbarians
or even uncultivated Greeks.   And it is
likely enough that the old man hankered
for the ease and comfort, for the atmosphere
of daily "spoiling," which the royal patron
was likely to provide for a lion of such special
rarity.   For it must have been a little before
this time that Greece was ringing with a tale
of the value set on Euripides in distant and
hostile Sicily.   Seven thousand Athenians
had been made slaves in Syracuse after the
failure of the expedition; and the story now
came that some of them had been actually
granted their freedom because they were
able to recite speeches and choruses of
Euripides.   Apparently there was no book
trade between the warring cities; and the
Syracusans could only learn the great
poems by word of mouth.   Sicily and
Macedonia were proud to show that they
appreciated the highest poetry better than
Athens did.

It was a curious haven that Euripides
found.   In many ways Macedonia must
have been like a great fragment of that

Homeric or heroic age from which he had
drawn most of his stories. The scenery was
all on the grand scale. There were greater
plains and forests and rivers, wilder and
higher mountain ranges than in the rest of
Greece. And the people, though ruled by a
dynasty of Greek descent and struggling
up towards Hellenism, was still tribal, military and barbaric. A century later we hear
of the "old" Macedonian customs. A young
man might not dine at the men's tables till
he had killed his first wild boar. He had to
wear a leathern halter round his waist until
he had killed his first man. We hear that
when some Macedonian at the court made
a rude remark to Euripides the king straight-
way handed him over to the Athenian to be
scourged, a well-meant but embarrassing intervention. And the story told of Euripides' own death, if mythical, is very likely
faithful in its local colour. There was a
village in Macedonia where some Thracians
had once settled and their descendants still
lived. One of the king's big Molossian
hounds once strayed into this place, and the
natives promptly killed and ate her. The
king fined the village a talent, which was
more than it could possibly pay, and some
dreadful fate might have overtaken the dog-

eaters had not Euripides interceded and
begged them off. And not long afterwards,
the story continues, Archelaus was preparing a hunt, and the hungry hounds were set
loose. And it so happened that Euripides
was sitting alone in a wood outside the city,
and the hounds fell on him and tore him to
pieces. And behold, these hounds proved
to be the children of that Molossian who,
through the poet's interference, had died
unavenged! The story can hardly be true,
or we should hear some echo of it in Aristophanes' *Frogs;* but no doubt it was the kind
of fate that a lonely man might well meet in
Macedonia when the king's hounds were
astir.

How the poet really died we do not
know. We know that he left Athens after
the spring of 408, and that he was dead
some time before the production of `the
Frogs in January, 405. And there is reason
to believe the story given in the Life that
when Sophocles in the previous year was
introducing his Chorus in the "Proagon,"
or Preliminary Appearance, he brought
them on without the customary garlands
in mourning for his great rival's death.
The news, therefore, must have reached
Athens by the end of March, 406. Euripi-

des had lived only some eighteen months
in Macedon.

The time was not long but it was momentous. After his death three plays were
found, *Iphigenia in Aulis*, *Alcmaeon* and
Bacchae, sufficiently finished to be put on
the stage together by his third son, the
Younger Euripides. Two of them are still
extant, and one, the *Bacchae*, remains for
all time to testify to the extraordinary
return of youth which came to the old poet
in his last year. A "lightning before death"
if ever there was one!

But let's take first the *Iphigenia in Aulis*.
It is a play full of problems. We can make
out that it was seriously incomplete at the
poet's death and was finished by another
hand, presumably that of its producer. Unfortunately we do not possess even that
version in a complete form. For the arche-
type of our MSS. was at some time mutilated,
and the present end of the play is a patent
forgery. But if we allow for these defects,
the *Iphigenia in Aulis* is a unique and most
interesting example of a particular moment
in the history of Greek drama. It shows
the turning-point between the old fifth century tragedy and the so-called New Comedy
which, in the hands of Menander, Philemon

and others, dominated the stage of the fourth
and third centuries.

Euripides had united two tendencies: on
the one hand he had moved towards freedom
in metre, realism in character-drawing,
variety and adventure in the realm of plot;
on the other he had strongly maintained the
formal and musical character of the old
Dionysiac ritual, making full use of such
conventions as the Prologue, the Epiphany,
the traditional tragic diction, and above all
the Chorus. The New Comedy dropped the
chorus, brought the diction close to real
life, broke up the stiff forms and revelled in
romance, variety, and adventure. Its characters ceased to be legendary Kings and
Queens; they became fictional characters
from ordinary city life.

The *Iphigenia in Aulis* shows an un-
finished Euripidean tragedy, much in the
manner of the *Orestes*, completed by a man
of some genius whose true ideals were those
of modernity and the New Comedy. Two
openings of the play are preserved. One is
the old stiff Euripidean prologue; the other
a fine and vigorous scene of lyric dialogue,
which must have suited the taste of the time
far better, just as it suits our own. We
have early in the play a Messenger; but in-

stead of his entrance being formally prepared and announced in the Euripidean
manner, he bursts on to the stage interrupt-
ing a speaker in the middle of a verse and
the middle of a sentence.   There are also
peculiarities of metre, such as the elision of
-ai, which are unheard of in tragic dialogue
but regular in the more conversational style
of the New Comedy.

The plot runs thus.—It is night in the
Greek camp at Aulis; Agamemnon calls an
Old Slave outside his tent and gives him
secretly a letter to carry to Clytemnestra.
She is at home, and has been directed in
previous letters to send her daughter,
Iphigenîa, to Aulis to be wedded to Achilles.
This letter simply bids her not send the girl.
—The Old Slave is bewildered; "What does
it mean?" It means that the marriage with
Achilles was a blind. Achilles knew nothing of it. It was a plot to get Iphigenîa to
the camp and there slaughter her as a sacrifice for the safe passage of the fleet. So
Calchas, the priest, had commanded and he
was backed by Odysseus and Menelaus.
Agamemnon had been forced into com-
pliance, and is now resolved to go back upon
his word. The Old Slave goes. Presently
comes the entrance of the Chorus, women of

Aulis who are dazzled and thrilled by the
spectacle of the great army and the men who
are prepared to die overseas for the honour
of Hellas.   But we hear a scuffle outside,
and the Old Slave returns pursued by Menelaus, who seizes the letter.   He calls for help.
Agamemnon comes out and commands Menelaus to give the letter back.   A violent scene
ensues between the brothers, each telling
the other home truths.   Menelaus's besotted
love for his false wife, his reckless selfishness
and cruelty; Agamemnon's consuming ambition, his falseness and weakness, his wish
to run with the hare and hunt with the
hounds, are all laid bare in a masterly quarrel
scene.   At last Agamemnon flatly refuses to
give his daughter: "Let the army break up,
let Menelaus go without his accursed wife,
and the barbarians laugh as loudly as they
will!   Agamemnon will not have his child
slain and his own heart broken to please any
one."   "Is that so?" says Menelaus: "Then
I go straight to. . . ."   He is interrupted by
a Messenger who announces that Iphigenîa
has come and her mother, Clytemnestra, is
with her.   Agamemnon sends them a formal
message of welcome; dismisses the Messenger, and then bursts into tears.   This
shakes Menelaus; he hesitates; then abruptly

says, "I cannot force you. Save the girl as
best you can." But now it is too late. The
army knows that the Queen has come; Calchas and Odysseus know. Agamemnon has
lost the power of action. The next scene is
between the mother, father and daughter;
Clytemnestra, full of questions about the
marriage, Iphigenia full of excitement and
shy tenderness, which expresses itself in
special affectionateness towards her father.
He tries to persuade Clytemnestra to go
home and leave the child with him; she is
perplexed and flatly refuses to go.

The next scene is close to comedy, though
comedy of a poignant kind. Achilles, knowing naught of all these plots and counter-
plots, comes to tell the General that his
men—the Myrmidons—are impatient and
want to sail for Troy at once. At the door
of the tent he meets Clytemnestra, who
greets him with effusive pleasure and speaks
of "the marriage that is about to unite
them." The young soldier is shy, horrified,
anxious to run away from this strange lady
who is so more than friendly, when suddenly a whisper through the half-closed door
startles them. "Is the coast clear? Yes?"
—then the whisperer will come. It is the Old
Slave, who can bear it no more but reveals the

whole horrible plot; Iphigenía is to be slaugh-
tered by the priests; the marriage with
Achilles was a bait for deceiving Clytemnestra.—Clytemnestra is thunderstruck,
Achilles furious with rage. "He is dishonoured; he is made a fool of. What sort
of man do they take him for, to use his name
thus without his authority? Why could not
they ask his consent? They could sacrifice
a dozen girls for all he cares, and he would
not have stood in the way. But now they
have dishonoured him, and he will forbid
the sacrifice. . . ." Clytemnestra, who has
watched like a drowning woman to see which
way the youth's fierce vanity would leap,
throws herself at his feet in gratitude;
"Shall her daughter, also, come and
embrace his knees?" No; Achilles does
not want any woman to kneel to him. Let
the women try to change Agamemnon's
mind; if they can do it, all is well. If
not, Achilles will fight to the last to save
the girl.

There follows the inevitable scene in which
mother and daughter—the latter inarticulate with tears—convict the father and
appeal to him. A fine scene it is, in
which each character comes out clear,
and through the still young and obedient

Clytemnestra one descries the shadow of
the great murderess to be. Agamemnon
is broken but helpless. It is too late to go
back.

The two women are left weeping at the
door of the tent, when they hear a sound of
tumult. It is Achilles, and men behind
stoning him. Iphigenía's first thought is to
fly; she dare not look Achilles in the face.
Yet she stays. Achilles enters. The whole
truth has come out; the army clamours for
the sacrifice and is furious against him. . . .
"Will not his own splendid Myrmidons protect him?"—"It is they who were the first
to stone him! Nevertheless he will fight.
He has his arms. Clytemnestra must fight
too; cling to her daughter by main force
when they come, as they presently will, to
drag her to the altar. . . ." "Stay!" says
Iphigenía: "Achilles must not die for her
sake. What is her miserable life compared
with his? One man who can fight for Hellas
is worth ten thousand women, who can do
nothing. Besides, she has been thinking it
over; she has seen the great gathered army,
ready to fight and die for a cause, and, like
the Chorus, has fallen under the spell of it.
She realizes that it lies with her, a weak girl,
to help them to victory. All great Hellas is

looking to her; and she is proud and glad to
give her life for Hellas."—It is a beautiful
and simple speech. And the pride of Achilles
withers up before it. In a new tone he answers: "God would indeed have made him
blessed if he had won her for his wife. As it
is, Iphigenia is right. . . ." Yet he offers
still to fight for her and save her. She does
not know what death is; and he loves her.—
She answers that her mind is made up. "Do
not die for me, but leave me to save Hellas,
if I can." Achilles yields. Still he will go
and stand beside the altar, armed; if at the
last moment she calls to him, he is ready. So
he goes. The mother and daughter bid one
another a last farewell, and with a song of
triumph Iphigenia, escorted by her maidens,
goes forth to meet the slaughterers. . . .
Here the authentic part of our play begins
to give out. There are fragments of a messenger's speech afterwards, and it is likely
on the whole that Artemis saved the
victim, as is assumed in the other *Iphigenia*
play.

The *Iphigenia in Aulis*, in spite of its good
plot, is not really one of Euripides' finest
works; yet, if nothing else of his were preserved, it would be enough to mark him out
as a tremendous power in the development

of Greek literature. Readers who enjoy
drama but have never quite accustomed
themselves to the stately conventions of
fifth century tragedy very often like it
better than any other Greek play. It is
curiously different from its twin sister the
Bacchae.

A reader of the *Bacchae* who looks back at
the ritual sequence described above (p. 63)
will be startled to find how close this drama,
apparently so wild and imaginative, has kept
to the ancient rite. The regular year-
sequence is just clothed in sufficient myth
to make it a story. The daemon must have
his enemy who is like himself; then we must
have the Contest, the Tearing Asunder, the
Messenger, the Lamentation mixed with Joy-
cries, the Discovery of the scattered members
—and by a sort of doubling the Discovery of
the true God—and the Epiphany of the
Daemon in glory. All are there in the *Bacchae.* The god Dionysus, accompanied by
his Wild Women, comes to his own land and
is rejected by his kinsman, King Pentheus,
and by the women of the royal house. The
god sends his divine madness on the women.
The wise Elders of the tribe warn the king;
but Pentheus first binds and imprisons the
god; then yielding gradually to the divine

power, agrees to go disguised in woman's garb to watch the secret worship of the Maenads on Mt. Kithairon. He goes, is discovered by the Maenads and torn in fragments. His mother, Agave, returns in triumph dancing with her son's head, which, in her madness, she takes for a lion's. There is Lamentation mixed with mad Rejoicing. The scattered body is recovered; Agave is restored to her right mind and to misery; the god appears in majesty and pronounces doom on all who have rejected him. The mortals go forth to their dooms, still faithful, still loving one another. The ghastly and triumphant god ascends into heaven. The whole scheme of the play is given by the ancient ritual. It is the original subject of Attic tragedy treated once more, as doubtless it had already been treated by all or almost all the other tragedians.

But we can go further. We have enough fragments and quotations from the Aeschylean plays on this subject—especially the Lycurgus trilogy—to see that all kinds of small details which seemed like invention, and rather fantastic invention, on the part of Euripides, are taken straight from Aeschylus or the ritual or both. The timbrels, the fawnskin, the ivy, the sacred pine, the god

taking the forms of Bull and Lion and Snake;
the dances on the mountain at dawn; the
Old Men who are by the power of the god
made young again; the god represented as
beardless and like a woman; the god imprisoned and escaping; the earthquake that
wrecks Pentheus' palace; the victim Pentheus disguised as a woman; all these and
more can be shown to be in the ritual and
nearly all are in the extant fragments of
Aeschylus. Even variants of the story which
have been used by previous poets have somehow a place found for them. There was, for
instance, a variant which made Pentheus
lead an army against the Wild Women; in
the *Bacchae* this plan is not used, but Pentheus is made to think of it and say he will
perhaps follow it, and Dionysus is made to
say what will happen if he does. (*Aesch.
Eum.* 25 f.; *Bac.* 50 ff. 809, 845.) There
never was a great play so steeped in tradition as the *Bacchae*.

The *Iphigenia* was all invention, construction, brilliant psychology; it was a play of
new plot and new characters. The *Bacchae*
takes an old fixed plot, and fixed formal
characters: Dionysus, Pentheus, Cadmus,
Teiresias, they are characters that hardly
need proper names. One might just as well

call them—The God, the Young King, the
Old King, the Prophet; and as for Agave,
our MSS. do as a rule simply call her
"Woman." The *Iphigenia* is full of infor-
malities, broken metres, interruptions. Its
Chorus hardly matters to the plot and has
little to sing. The *Bacchae* is the most formal
Greek play known to us; its Chorus is its
very soul and its lyric songs are as long as
they are magnificent. For the curious thing
is that in this extreme of formality and faith-
fulness to archaic tradition Euripides has
found both his greatest originality and his
most perfect freedom.

He is re-telling an old story; but he is not
merely doing that. In the *Bacchae* almost
every reader feels that there is something
more than a story. There is a meaning, or
there is at least a riddle. And we must try
in some degree to understand it. Now, in
order to keep our heads cool, it is first necessary to remember clearly two things. The
Bacchae is not free invention; it is tradition.
And it is not free personal expression, it is
drama. The poet cannot simply and without a veil state his own views; he can only
let his own personality shine through the
dim curtain in front of which his puppets
act their traditional parts and utter their

appropriate sentiments. Thus it is doubly
elusive. And therein no doubt lay its charm
to the poet. He had a vehicle into which he
could pour many of those "vaguer faiths
and aspirations which a man feels haunting
him and calling to him, but which he cannot state in plain language or uphold with a
full acceptance of responsibility." But our
difficulties are even greater than this. The
personal meaning of a drama of this sort is
not only elusive; it is almost certain to be
inconsistent with itself or at least incomplete. For one only feels its presence strongly
when in some way it clashes with the smooth
flow of the story.

Let us imagine a great free-minded modern
poet—say Swinburne or Morris or Victor
Hugo, all of whom did such things—making
for some local anniversary a rhymed play in
the style of the old Mysteries on some legend
of a mediæval saint. The saint, let us suppose, is very meek and is cruelly persecuted
by a wicked emperor, whom he threatens
with hell fire; and at the end let us have the
emperor in the midst of that fire and the
saint in glory saying, "What did I tell you?"
And let us suppose that the play in its course
gives splendid opportunities for solemn Latin
hymns, such as Swinburne and Hugo delighted

in.   We should probably have a result something like the *Bacchae*.

For one thing, in such a play one would
not be troubled by little flaws and anachro-
nisms and inconsistencies. One would not be
shocked to hear St. Thomas speaking about
Charlemagne, or to find the Mouth of Hell
situated in the same street as the emperor's
lodging. Just so we need not be shocked in
the *Bacchae* to find that, though the god is
supposed to be appearing for the first time
in Thebes, his followers appeal to "immemo-
rial custom" as the chief ground for their worship (201, 331, 370: cf. *Aesch.* fr. 22?), nor
to observe that the Chorus habitually makes
loud professions of faith under the very nose
of the tyrant without his ever attending to
them (263 f., 328 f., 775 f.). Nor even that
the traditional earthquake which destroys
the palace causes a good deal of trouble in
the thinking out. It had to be there; it was
an integral part of the story in Aeschylus
(fr. 58), and in all probability before him.
One may suppose that the Greek stage car-
penter was capable of some symbolic crash
which served its purpose. The language
used is carefully indefinite. It suggests that
the whole palace is destroyed, but leaves a
spectator free, if he so chooses, to suppose

that it is only the actual prison of Dionysus, which is "off-stage" and unseen. In any case the ruins are not allowed to litter the stage and, once over, the earthquake is never noticed or mentioned again.

Again, such a play would involve a bewildering shift of sympathy, just as the *Bacchae* does. At first we should be all for the saint and against the tyrant; the persecuted monks with their hymns of faith and endurance would stir our souls. Then, when the tables were turned and the oppressors were seen writhing in Hell, we should feel that, at their worst, they did not quite deserve that: we should even begin to surmise that perhaps, with all their faults, they were not really as horrible as the saint himself, and reflect inwardly what a barbarous thing, after all, this mediæval religion was.

This bewildering shift of sympathy is common in Euripides. We have had it before in such plays as the *Medea* and *Hecuba:* oppression generates revenge, and the revenge becomes more horrible than the original oppression. In these plays the poet offers no solution. He gives us only the bitterness of life and the unspoken "tears that are in things." The first serious attempt at a solution comes in the *Electra* and *Orestes.*

In a Mystery-play such as we have imagined, re-told by a great modern poet, the
interest and meaning would hardly lie in the
main plot. They would lie in something
which the poet himself contributed. We
might, for instance, find that he had poured
all his soul into the Latin hymns, or into the
spectacle of the saint, alone and unterrified,
defying all the threats and all the temptations
which the Emperor can bring to bear upon
him. There might thus be a glorification of
that mystic rejection of the world which lies
at the heart of mediæval monasticism, without the poet˙ for a moment committing
himself to a belief in monasticism or an
acceptance of the Catholic Church.

We have in the *Bacchae*—it seems to me
impossible to deny it—a heartfelt glorification of "Dionysus." No doubt it is Dionysus
in some private sense of the poet's own;
something opposed to "the world"; some
spirit of the wild woods and the sunrise, of
inspiration and untrammelled life. The presentation is not consistent, however magical
the poetry. At one moment we have the
Bacchantes raving for revenge, at the next
they are uttering the dreams of some gentle
and musing philosopher. A deliberate contrast seems to be made in each Chorus be-

tween the strophe and the antistrophe. It
is not consistent; though it is likely enough
that, if one had taxed Euripides with the
contradiction, he might have had some answer that would surprise us. His first de-
fence, of course, would be a simple one; it is
not the playwright's business to have any
views at all; he is only re-telling a traditional
story and trying to tell it right. But he
might also venture outside his defences and
answer more frankly: "This spirit that I call
Dionysus, this magic of inspiration and joy,
is it not as a matter of fact the great wrecker
of men's lives? While life seems a decent
grey to you all over, you are safe and likely
to be prosperous; when you feel the heavens
opening, you may begin to tremble. For the
vision you see there, as it is the most beautiful of things, is likely also to be the most
destructive." For the poet himself, indeed,
the only course is to pursue it across the
world or the cold mountain tops (410 ff.):

> For there is Grace, and there is the Heart's Desire,
> And peace to adore Thee, Thou spirit of guiding fire!

He will clasp it even though it slay him.
The old critics used to assume that the
Bacchae marked a sort of repentance. The
veteran free-lance of thought, the man who

had consistently denounced and ridiculed
all the foul old stories of mythology, now saw
the error of his ways and was returning to
orthodoxy. Such a view strikes us now as
almost childish incompetence. Yet there is,
I think, a gleam of muddled truth somewhere
behind it. There was no repentance; there
was no return to orthodoxy; nor indeed was
there, in the strict sense, any such thing as
"orthodoxy" to return to. For Greek religion had no creeds. But there is, I think,
a rather different attitude towards the pieties
of the common man.

It is well to remember that, for all his lucid-
ity of language, Euripides is not lucid about
religion. His general spirit is clear: it is a
spirit of liberation, of moral revolt, of much
denial; but it is also a spirit of search and
wonder and surmise. He was not in any sense
a "mere" rationalist. We find in his plays
the rule of divine justice often asserted, sometimes passionately denied; and one tragedy,
the *Bellerophontes*, is based on the denial. It
is in a fragment of this play that we have the
outcry of some sufferer:

> Doth any feign there is a God in heaven?
> There is none, none!

And afterwards the hero, staggered by the
injustice of things, questions Zeus himself

and is, for answer, blasted by the thunder-
bolt. A clearer form of this same question,
and one which vexed the age a good deal, was
to ask whether or no the world is governed by
some great Intelligence or Understanding
("*Sunesis*"), or, more crudely, whether the
gods are "*sunetoi*." Euripides at times "hath
deep in his hope a belief in some Understanding," and is represented in the *Frogs* as actually praying to it by that name; but he
sometimes finds the facts against him (*Hippolytus*, 1105; *Frogs*, 893; *Iph. Aul.*, 394a; *Her.*,
655; *Tro.*, 884 ff., compared with the sequel
of the play). The question between poly-
theism and monotheism, which has loomed so
large to some minds, never troubled him.
He uses the singular and plural quite indiffer-
ently, and probably his "gods," when used as
identical with "God" or "the Divine," would
hardly even suggest to him the gods of mythology. If one is to venture a conjecture,
his own feeling may, perhaps, be expressed
by a line in the *Orestes* (418):

We are slaves of gods, whatever gods may be.

That is, there are unknown forces which
shape or destroy man's life, and which may
be conceived as in some sense personal. But

morally, it would seem, these forces are not better, but less good, than man, who at least loves and pities and tries to understand. Such is the impression, I think, left on readers of the *Bacchae*, the *Hippolytus* or the *Trojan Women*.

But there is one thought which often recurs in Euripides in plays of all periods, and is specially thrown in his teeth by Aristophanes. That satirist, when piling up Euripides' theatrical iniquities, takes as his comic climax "women who say Life is not Life." The reference is to passages like fr. 833, from the *Phrixus:*

> Who knoweth if the thing that we call death
> Be Life, and our Life dying—who knoweth?
> Save only that all we beneath the sun
> Are sick and suffering, and those foregone
> Not sick, nor touched with evil any more.

(*Cf.* fr. 638, 816; also *Helena*, 1013; *Frogs*, 1082, 1477.) The idea recurs again and again, as also does the thought that death is "some other shape of life" in the *Medea* and even in the *Ion* (*Med.*, 1039; *Ion*, 1068). Nay, more, death may be the state that we unconsciously long for, and that really fulfils our inmost desires: "There is no rest on this earth," says a speaker in the *Hippolytus* (191 f.),

And whatever far-off state there be,
Dearer than Life to mortality,
The hand of the Dark hath hold thereof
And mist is under and mist above:

Noah's waters above + below The firmament.

and thus," she continues, "we cling to this
strange thing that shines in the sunlight,
and are sick with love for it, because we
have not seen beyond the veil." A stirring
thought this, and much nearer to the heart
of mysticism than any mere assertion of
human immortality. Thus it is not from
any position like what we should call "dog-
matic atheism" or "scientific materialism"
that the child of the Sophists started his
attacks on the current mythology. The
Sophists themselves had no orthodoxy. ——

Euripides was always a rejecter of the
Laws of the Herd. He was in protest against
its moral standards, its superstitions and
follies, its social injustices; in protest also
against its worldliness and its indifference
to those things which, both as a poet and a
philosopher, he felt to be highest. And
such he remained throughout his life. But
in his later years the direction of his protest
did, I think, somewhat change. In the
Athens of Melos and the Sicilian expedition
there was something that roused his aversion far more than did the mere ignorance of

a stupid Greek farmer. It was a deeper
"*amathia*," a more unteachable brutality.
The men who spoke in the Melian Dialogue
were full of what they considered "Sophia."
It is likely enough that they conformed carefully to the popular religious prejudices—
such politicians always do: but in practice
they thought as little of "the gods" as the
most pronounced sceptic could wish. They
had quite rejected such unprofitable ideals
as "pity and charm of words and the generosity of strength," to which the simple
man of the old times had always had the
door of his heart open. They were haunters
of the market-place, mockers at all simplicity, close pursuers of gain and revenge;
rejecters, the poet might feel in his bitterness, both of beauty and of God. And the
Herd, as represented by Athens, followed
them. Like other ideal democrats he turned
away from the actual Demos, which surrounded him and howled him down, to a
Demos of his imagination, pure and uncor-
rupted, in which the heart of the natural man
should speak. His later plays break out
more than once into praises of the unspoiled
countryman, neither rich nor poor, who
works with his own arm and whose home is
"the   solemn   mountain" not   the   city

streets (*cf.* especially *Orestes*, 917–922, as contrasted with 903 ff.; also the Peasant in the *Electra;* also *Bac.*, 717). In the *Bacchae* we have not only several denunciations— not at all relevant to the main plot—of those whom the world calls "wise"; we have the wonderful chorus about the fawn escaped from the hunters, rejoicing in the green and lonely places where no pursuing voice is heard and the "little things of the woodland" live unseen. (866 ff.) That is the poetry of this emotion. The prose of it comes in a sudden cry:

> The simple nameless herd of humanity
> Have deeds and faith that are truth enough for me;

though even that prose has followed immediately on the more mystical doctrine that man must love the Day and the Night, and that Dionysus has poured the mystic Wine that is Himself for all things that live (421–431, 284). In another passage, which I translate literally, he seems to make his exact position more clear: "As for Knowledge, I bear her no grudge; I take joy in the pursuit of her. But the other things" (*i.e.*, the other elements of existence) "are great and shining. Oh, for Life to flow towards that which is beautiful, till man through both light and darkness should be at peace and reverent, and, casting from him Laws that are outside Justice, give glory to the gods!" [1]

Those "Laws which are outside Justice" would make trouble enough between Euripides and the "simple herd" if ever they reached the point of discussing them. He who most loves the ideal Natural Man seldom agrees with the majority of his neighbours. But for the meantime the poet is wrapped up in another war, in which he and religion and nature and the life of the simple man seem to be standing on one side against a universal enemy.

I am not attempting to expound the whole meaning of the *Bacchae*. I am only suggesting a clue by which to follow it. Like a live thing it seems to move and show new faces every time that, with imagination fully working, one reads the play. There were many factors at work, doubtless, to produce the *Bacchae*: the peculiar state of Athens, the poet's ecstasy of escape from an intolerable atmosphere, the simple Homeric

---

[1] In my verse translation I took a slightly different reading, being then misinformed about the MS., but the general sense is the same. ("Knowledge, we are not foes," etc.)

life in Macedonian forests and mountains, and perhaps even the sight of real Bacchantes dancing there. But it may be that the chief factor is simply this. When a man is fairly confronted with death and is consciously doing his last work in the world, the chances are that, if his brain is clear and unterrified, the deepest part of his nature will assert itself. Euripides was both a reasoner and a poet. The two sides of his nature sometimes clashed and sometimes blended. But ever since the *Heracles* he had known which service he really lived for; and in his last work it is the poet who speaks, and reveals, so far as such a thing can be revealed, the secret religion of poetry.

CHAPTER VIII

THE ART OF EURIPIDES: IDEAL FORM AND SINCERE SPIRIT: PROLOGUE: MESSENGER: "DEUS EX MÂCHINÂ"

EURIPIDES was so much besides a poet that we sometimes tend to regard him exclusively as a great thinker or a great personality and forget that it is in his poetry that he lives. A biography like that which we have attempted to sketch is of little value except as a kind of clue to guide a reader through the paths of the poet's own work. It is only by reading his plays that we can know him; and unfortunately, owing to the two thousand odd years that have passed since his death, we must needs approach them through some distorting medium. We read them either in a foreign language, as a rule most imperfectly understood, or else in a translation. It is hard to say by which method a reader who is not a quite good Greek scholar will miss most. A further difficulty occurs about the translations. I need not perhaps apologize for assuming normally in the pres-

196

ent volume the use of my own.   There has
been lately, since the work of Verrall in England and Wilamowitz in Germany, a far
more successful effort made to understand
the mind of Euripides, while the recent per-
formances of his plays in London and elsewhere have considerably increased our insight into his stagecraft.   Consequently we
can now see that the older translations, even
when verbally defensible and even skilful,
are often seriously inadequate or misleading.   A comparison of Dr. Verrall's English
version of the *Ion* with practically any of its
predecessors will illustrate this point.

The greatest change that has come over
our study of Greek civilization and literature in the last two generations is this: that
we now try to approach it historically, as a
thing that moves and grows and has its place
in the whole life-history of man.   The old
view, sometimes called classicist, was to regard the great classical books as eternal
models; their style was simply the right
style, and all the variations observable in
modern literature were, in one degree or
another, so many concessions to the weakness of human nature.   There is in this
view an element of truth.   The fundamental
ideals which have produced results so singu-

larly and so permanently successful cannot
be lightly disregarded. Books that are still
read with delight after two thousand years
are certainly, in some sense, models to imi-
tate. But the great flaw in the classicist
view, as regards the ancient literature itself,
was that it concentrated attention on the
external and accidental; on the mannerism,
not the meaning; on the temporary fashion of
a great age, not on, the spirit which made
that age great. A historical mind will always
try, by active and critical use of the imagination, to see the Greek poet or philosopher in
his real surroundings and against his proper
background. Seen thus he will appear, not
as a stationary "ancient" contrasted with
a "modern," but as a moving and striving
figure, a daring pioneer in the advance of
the human spirit, fore-doomed to failure
because his aims were so far greater than
his material resources, his habit of mind so
far in advance of the world that surrounded
him. We seem in ancient Greece to be moving in a region that is next door to savagery,
and in the midst of it to have speech with
men whom we might gladly accept as our
leaders or advisers if they lived now.

Meantime there are screens between us
and these men; the screens of a foreign lan-

guage, a strange form of life, different conventions in art. It is these last that we must now deal with, for we shall find it hard ever to understand Greek tragedy if we expect from it exactly what we expect from a modern or Elizabethan play.

One would have to make no such preface if we were dealing with the form of Greek Drama that immediately succeeded the great age of Tragedy. There arose in the fourth century, B.C., a kind of play that we could understand at once, the so-called New Comedy of Menander and Philemon. New Comedy is neither tragic nor comic, but, like our own plays, a discreet mixture of both. It has no austere religious atmosphere. Its interest—like ours—is in love and adventure and intrigue. It has turned aside from legend and legendary Kings and Queens, and operates, as we do, with a boldly invented plot and fictitious characters, drawn mostly from everyday life. The New Comedy dominated the later Attic stage and called into life the Roman. It was highly praised and immensely popular. It was so easy in 'its flow and it demanded so little effort. Yet, significantly enough, it has passed away without leaving a single complete specimen of its work in existence.

When after ages were exerting themselves
to save from antiquity just that minimum
of most precious things that must not be
allowed to die, it was the greater and
more difficult form of drama that they
preserved.

Let us try to see and to surmount the
difficulties. Every form of art has its conventions. Think, for instance, of the conventions of modern Opera. Looked at in
cold blood, from outside the illusion, few
forms of art could be more absurd, yet, I
suppose, the emotional and artistic effect of
a great opera is extraordinarily high. The
analogy may help us in the understanding
of Greek tragedy.

Let us remember that it is at heart a religious ritual. We shall then understand—
so far as it is necessary for a modern reader
to think of such things—the ceremonial
dress, the religious masks, the constant
presence or nearness of the supernatural.
We shall understand, perhaps, also the formal
dignity of language and action. It is verse
and, like all Greek verse, unrhymed; but it
is not at all like the loose go-as-you-please
Elizabethan verse, which fluctuates from
scene to scene and makes up for its lack of
strict form by extreme verbal ornamenta-

tion. In Greek tragic dialogue the metrical
form is stiff and clear; hardly ever could a
tragic line by any mistake be taken for
prose; the only normal variation is not
towards prose but towards a still more
highly wrought musical lyric. Yet inside
the stiff metrical form the language is clear,
simple and direct. A similar effect can, in
my opinion, only be attained in English by
the use of rhyme. You must somehow feel
always that you are in the realm of verse, yet
your language must always be simple. In
blank verse the language has to be tortured
a little, or it will read like prose.

Now all this sounds highly conventional;
that it is. And artificial and unreal? That
it is not. We are apt at the present moment
of taste to associate together two things that
have no real connexion with one another—
sincerity of thought and sloppiness of form.
Take on the one hand dramatic poems like
Swinburne's *Locrine*, written all in rhymed
verse and partly in sonnets, or George Meredith's *Modern Love*, which is all in a form of
sonnet. These are works of the most highly-
wrought artistic convention; their form is
both severe and elaborate; in that lies half
their beauty. But the other half lies in their
sincerity and delicacy of thought and their

intensity of feeling. They are sincere but not
formless.   Of the other extreme, which is
formless without being sincere,'I need give no
examples. The reader can think of the worst-
written novel he knows and it will probably
satisfy the conditions.   In Greek tragedy we
have the element of formal convention ex-
tremely strong; we have also great subtlety
and sincerity.

This quality of sincerity is, perhaps, the
very first thing that should be pointed out to
a.reader who is beginning Greek tragedy.
Coming in the midst of so much poetical convention it takes a modern reader by surprise;
he expected romantic idealism and he finds
clear character-drawing. I once read a critic
who argued that Euripides had low ideals of
womanhood because, in the critic's carefully
pondered judgment, Medea was not a perfect
wife.   Even Coleridge complained that the
Greek tragedians could not make a heroine
interesting without "unsexing her."   Such
criticisms imply a conception of drama in
which the women are conventionally seen
through a roseate mist of amatory emotion.
We mean to be in love with the heroine, and
in order that she may be worthy of that honour the author must endow her with all the
adorable attributes.   The men in such

plays suffer much less from beautification, but even they suffer. This spurious
kind of romanticism implies chiefly an
indifference to truth in the realm of
character; it is generally accompanied by
an indifference to truth in other respects. It
leads stage-writers to look out for the effect,
not the truth; to write with a view to exciting
the audience instead of expressing something
which they have to express. It leads in fact
to all the forms of staginess. Now from
Greek tragedy this kind of falseness is almost entirely absent. "It has no utter villains, no insipidly angelic heroines. Even
its tyrants generally have some touch of human nature about them; they have at least
a case to state. Even its virgin martyrs are
not waxen images." The stories are no
doubt often miraculous; the characters themselves are often in their origin supernatural.
But their psychology is severely true. It is
not the psychology of melodrama, specially
contrived to lead up to "situations." It is
that of observed human nature, and human
nature not merely observed but approached
with a serious almost reverent sympathy and
an unlimited desire to understand. Mr. Bernard Shaw, in his *Quintessence of Ibsenism*
(1913), writes of a new element brought into

modern drama by the Norwegian school. "Ibsen was grim enough in all conscience; no man has said more terrible things; and yet there is not one of Ibsen's characters who is not, in the old phrase, the temple of the Holy Ghost, and who does not move you at moments by the sense of that mystery." Allowing for the great difference of treatment and the comparative absence of detail in the ancient drama, this phrase would, I think, be true of all the great Greek tragedians. In Euripides it is clear enough. Jason, as well as Medea, Clytemnestra as well as Electra, even satirized characters like Menelaus in the *Trojan Women* or Agamemnon in the *Iphigenîa in Aulis*, are creatures of one blood with ourselves; they are beings who must be understood, who cannot be thrust beyond the pale; and they all "move us at moments by the sense of that mystery." But it holds in general for the other tragedians too, for the creators of Creon and Antigone, of Prometheus and Zeus. "What poet until quite modern times would have dared to make an audience sympathize with Clytemnestra, the bloodstained adulteress, as Aeschylus does? Who would have dared, like Sophocles, to make Antigone speak cruelly to her devoted sister, or Electra, with all our sympathies concentrated upon her, behave like a wild beast and be disgusted with herself for so doing? (*Soph. Elec.* 616 ff.).''

But what we have now to realize is that this sincerity of treatment takes place inside a shell of stiff and elaborate convention.

At the very beginning of a play by Euripides we shall find something that seems deliberately calculated to offend us and destroy our interest: a Prologue. It is a long speech with no action to speak of; and it tells us not only the present situation of the characters— which is rather dull—but also what is going to happen to them—which seems to us to spoil the rest of the play. And the modern scholastic critic says in his heart, "Euripides had no sense of the stage."

Now, since we know that he had a very great sense of the stage and enormous experience also, let us try to see what value he found in this strange prologue. First, no doubt it was a convenience. There were no playbills to hand round, with lists of the *dramatis personae*. Also, a Greek tragedy is always highly concentrated; it consists generally of what would be the fifth act of a modern tragedy, and does not spend its time on explanatory and introductory acts. The Pro-

logue saved time here. But why does it let
out the secret of what is coming? Why does
it spoil the excitement beforehand? Because,
we must answer, there is no secret, and the
poet does not aim at that sort of excitement.
A certain amount of plot-interest there certainly is: we are never told exactly what
thing will happen but only what sort of thing;
or we are told what will happen but not how
it will happen. But the enjoyment which the
poet aims at is not the enjoyment of reading
a detective story for the first time; it is that
of reading *Hamlet* or *Paradise Lost* for the
second or fifth or tenth. When Hippolytus
or Oedipus first appears on the stage you
know that he is doomed; that knowledge
gives an increased significance to everything
that he says or does; you see the shadow of
disaster closing in behind him, and when
the catastrophe comes it comes with the
greater force because you were watching
for it.

"At any rate," the modern reader may
persist: "the prologue is rather dull. It does
not arrest the attention, like, for instance, the
opening scenes of *Macbeth* or *Julius Caesar*
or *Romeo and Juliet*." No; it does not.
Shakespeare, one may suppose, had a somewhat noisy audience, all talking among

themselves and not disposed to listen till
their attention was captured by force. The
Greek audience was, as far as we can make
out, sitting in a religious silence. A prayer
had been offered and incense burnt on the
altar of Dionysus, and during such a ritual
the rule enjoined silence. It was not necessary for the Greek poet to capture his audience by a scene of bustle or excitement.
And this left him free to do two things,
both eminently characteristic of Greek
art. He could make his atmosphere and
he could build up his drama from the
ground.

Let us take the question of building first.
If you study a number of modern plays, you
will probably find that their main "effects"
are produced in very different places, though
especially of course at the fall of each curtain. A good Greek play moves almost always
in a curve of steadily increasing tension—increasing up to the last scene but one and then,
as a rule, sinking into a note of solemn calm.
It often admits a quiet scene about the middle to let the play take breath; but it is very
chary indeed of lifting and then dropping
again, and never does so without definite
reason. In pursuance of this plan, Euripides likes to have his opening as low-toned,

as still, as slow in movement, as he can make
it: its only tension is a feeling of foreboding
or of mystery. It is meant as a foundation to build upon, and every scene that
follows will be higher, swifter, more intense. A rush of excitement at the opening
would jar, so to speak, the whole musical
scheme.

And this quiet opening is especially used
to produce the right state of mind in the
audience—or, as our modern phrase puts it,
to give the play its atmosphere. Take almost any opening: the *Suppliant Women*,
with its band of desolate mothers kneeling at
an altar and holding the Queen prisoner
while she speaks: the *Andromache*, the *Heracles*, the *Children of Heracles* almost the same
—an altar and helpless people kneeling at it
—kneeling and waiting: the *Trojan Women*
with its dim-seen angry gods; the *Hecuba*
with its ruined city walls and desolate plain
and the ghost of the murdered Polydorus
brooding over them; the *Hippolytus* with its
sinister goddess, potent and inexorable, who
vanishes at the note of the hunting horn but
is felt in the background throughout the
whole play; the *Iphigenia*, with its solitary
and exiled priestess waiting at the doors of
her strange temple of death. Most of the

prologues have about them something supernatural; all of them something mysterious; and
all of them are scenes of waiting, not acting
—waiting till the atmosphere can slowly
gain its full hold. Regarded from this point
of view I think that every opening scene in
Greek tragedy will be seen to have its significance and its value in the whole scheme of
the play. Certainly the prologue generally
justifies itself in the acting.

And when the prologue is over and the action begins, we need not expect even then any
rapid stir or bustle. Dr. Johnson has told
us that a man who should read Richardson
for the story might as well hang himself; the
same fate might overtake one who sate at
Greek tragedies expecting them to hurry at
his bidding. The swift rush will come, sure
enough, swift and wild with almost intolerable passion; but it will not come anywhere
near the first scenes. We shall have a dialogue in longish speeches, each more or less
balanced against its fellow, beautiful no
doubt and perhaps moving, but slow as music is slow. Or we shall have a lyrical scene,
strophe exactly balanced against antistrophe, more beautiful but slower still in its
movement, and often at first hearing a little

difficult to follow. Poetry is there and drama is there, and character and plot interest; but often they are unrolled before you not as things immediately happening, but as things to feel and reflect upon. It is a bigger world than ours and every movement in it is slower and larger.

And when the poet wants to show us the heroine's state of mind his method will be quite different from ours. We should rack our brains to compose a "natural" dialogue in which her state of mind would appear, or we should make her best friend explain what she is like, or we should invent small incidents to throw light upon her. And our language would all the time be carefully naturalistic; not a bit—or, if the poet within us rebels, hardly a bit—more dignified than the average diction of afternoon tea. The ancient poet has no artifice at all. His heroine simply walks forward and explains her own feelings. But she will come at some moment that seems just the right one; she will come to us through a cloud, as it were, of musical emotion from the Chorus, and her words when she speaks will be frankly the language of poetry. They will be none the less sincere or exact for that.

When Phaedra in the *Hippolytus* has re-

solved to die rather than show her love,
much less attempt to satisfy it, and yet
has been so weakened by her long struggle
that she will not be able to resist much
longer, she explains herself to the Chorus in a
long speech:

> O Women, dwellers in this portal seat
> Of Pelops' land, looking towards my Crete,
> How oft, in other days than these, have I
> Through night's long hours thought of man's misery
> And how this life is wrecked! And, to mine eyes,
> Not in man's knowledge, not in wisdom, lies
> The lack that makes for sorrow. Nay, we scan
> And know the right—for wit hath many a man—
> But will not to the last end strive and serve.
> For some grow too soon weary, and some swerve
> To other paths, setting before the right
> The diverse far-off image of Delight,
> And many are delights beneath the sun. . . .

It is not the language that any real woman
ever spoke, and it is not meant to be. But
it is exactly the thought which this woman
may have thought and felt, transmuted into
a special kind of high poetry. And the women
of the Chorus who are listening to it are like
no kind of concrete earthly listeners; they
are the sort of listeners that are suited to
thoughts rather than words, and their own
answer at the end comes not like a real comment but like a note of music. When she

finishes, defending her resolve to die rather
than sin:

> O'er all this earth
> To every false man that hour comes apace
> When Time holds up a mirror to his face,
> And marvelling, girl-like, there he stares to see
> How foul his heart.—Be it not so with me!

They answer:

> Ah, God, how sweet is virtue and how wise,
> And honour its due meed in all men's eyes!

"A commonplace?" "A not very original
remark?" There is no need for any original
remark; what is needed is a note of harmony
in words and thought, and that is what we are
given.

At a later stage in the play we shall come
on another fixed element in the tragedy, the
Messenger's Speech. It was probably in the
ritual. It was expected in the play. And
it was—and is still on the stage—immensely
dramatic and effective. Modern writers like
Mr. Masefield and Mr. Wilfred Blunt have
seen what use can be made of a Messenger's
speech. Now for the understanding of the
speech itself, what is needed is to read it
several times, to mark out exactly the stages

of story told, and the gradual rising of emotion and excitement up to the highest point,
which is, as usual, near the end but not at the
end. The end sinks back to something like
calm. It would take too long to analyse a
particular Messenger's speech paragraph by
paragraph, and the printed page cannot, of
course, illustrate the constant varieties of tension, of pace and of emphasis that are needed.
But I find the following notes for the guidance
of an actor opposite the Messenger's Speech
in an old copy of my *Hippolytus*. Opposite
the first lines comes, "Quiet, slow, simple."
Then "quicker." "Big" (at "O Zeus . . .
hated me"). Then "Drop tension: story."
"Pause: more interest." "Mystery." "Awe;
rising excitement." "Excitement well controlled." "Steady excitement; steady;
swifter." "Up: excitement rising." "Up; but
still controlled." "Up; full steam; let it go."
"Highest point." "Down to quiet." "Mystery." "Pause." "End steady: with emotion." These notes have, of course, no
authority: as they stand they are due partly
to my own conjecture, partly to observation
of a remarkable performance. But they
have this interest about them. They grow
out of the essential nature of the speech and
probably would, in their general tenour, be

accepted by most students; and further, some very similar scheme would suit not only almost every Messenger's speech, but also, with the necessary modifications, almost every Greek tragedy as a whole. The quiet beginning, the constant rise of tension through various moods and various changes of tone up to a climax; the carefully arranged drop from the climax to the steady close, without bathos and without any wrecking of the continuity.

But there is another point about Messengers that can be more easily illustrated. Their entrance in Euripides is nearly always carefully prepared. The point is of cardinal importance and needs some explanation. In mere literature it is the words that matter; in dramatic literature it is partly the words, and partly the situation in which they are uttered. A Messenger's speech ought not only to be a good story in itself, but it ought to be so prepared and led up to that before the speaker begins we are longing to hear what he has to say. An instance of a Messenger's speech with no preparation is in Sophocles' *Oedipus, The King*. (I do not at all suggest that preparation is needed; very likely the situation itself is enough.) Oedipus has rushed into the house in a fury of despair, and the Messenger simply walks out of the house crying

O ye above this land in honour old
Exalted, what a tale shall ye be told,
What sights shall see and tears of horror shed. . . .

Contrast with this the preparation in the *Hippolytus* (1153 ff.). Hippolytus, cursed, and of course, wrongfully cursed, by his father, Theseus, has gone forth to exile. His friends and the women of the Chorus have been grieving for him: Theseus has refused to listen to any plea. Then

LEADER OF THE CHORUS
Look yonder! . . . Surely from the Prince 'tis one
That cometh, full of haste and woe-begone.

We are all watching; a man in great haste enters. Observe what he says.

HENCHMAN
Ye women, whither shall I go to seek
King Theseus? Is he in this dwelling? Speak!

Our suspense deepens. The Leader evidently has hesitated in her answer; she wants to ask a question. . . . But at this moment the door opens and she falls back:

LEADER
Lo, where he cometh through the Castle Gate.

Through the gate comes Theseus, wrapped in
gloom, evidently trying still to forget Hippolytus.   The Henchman crosses his path.

HENCHMAN

O King, I bear thee tidings of dire weight
To thee, yea, and to every man, I ween,
From Athens to the marshes of Trozên.

Will Theseus guess?   Will he see that this is
one of his son's servants?   At any rate he
shows no sign of so doing.

THESEUS

What?   Some new stroke hath touched, unknown to me
The sister cities of my sovranty?

HENCHMAN

Hippolytus is. . . . Nay, not dead; but stark
Outstretched, a hairsbreadth this side of the dark.

The forbidden name is spoken; there is evidently a moment of shock, but how will Theseus take the news?   Will he soften?

THESEUS (*as though unmoved*)

How slain?   Was there some other man, whose wife
He had like mine defiled, who sought his life?

Stung by the taunt the Henchman answers
coldly.

HENCHMAN

His own wild team destroyed him, and the dire
Curse of thy lips. . . . The boon of the great Sire
Is granted thee, O King, and thy son slain.

Will Theseus turn in fury on the speaker?
Or will he even now soften?   Neither.

THESEUS

Ye Gods! . . . And thou, Poseidon, not in vain
I called thee Father.   Thou hast heard my prayer.

The shock is heavy but he recovers his calm,
and with it comes the horrible conviction that
his curse was just and the gods have struck
dead a guilty man.

How did he die?   Speak on.   How closed the snare
Of Heaven to slay the shamer of my blood?

Then the Messenger begins his story.

Such preparations are regular in Euripides.
In the *Electra*, Orestes has gone forth to find
King Aegisthus, and if possible slay him.
Electra is waiting in her hut, a drawn sword
across her knees, sworn to die if Orestes fails.
How is the Messenger brought on?   First the
Leader of the Chorus thinks she hears a noise
in the distance; she is not sure. . . .   Yes; a
noise of fighting!   She calls Electra, who
comes, the sword in her hand.   The noise
increases; a cry; cheering.   Something has
happened, but what?   The cheers sound like
Argive voices;   "Aegisthus's men!" cries
Electra;   "then let me die!"   The Chorus
restrain her.   "There is no Messenger; Ores-

tes would have sent a Messenger." "Wait,
wait!" cries the Leader, holding her arm:
and a man rushes in, shouting, "Victory!
Orestes has slain Aegisthus, and we are free"
(747–773).

That seems enough, but even now Euripides has not extracted his full effect from
the situation. Electra, steeped to the lips in
fears and suspicions, recoils from the man.
"Who are you? . . . It is a plot!" She
must get the sword. . . . The Man bids her
look at him again; he is her brother's servant;
she saw him with Orestes an hour ago. She
looks, remembers, and throws her arms
round the man's neck. "Tell me again. Tell
me all that happened." And so the Messenger begins.

This art of preparation belongs, of course,
to the modern stage as much as to the ancient,
or more. So do the similar arts of making the
right juncture between scenes, of arranging
the contrasts and clashes, and especially of so
ending each scene as to make the spectator
look eagerly for the next move. He must be
given just enough notion of the future to
whet his appetite; not enough to satisfy it.
These are general rules that apply to all good
drama. They can all be studied in Mr.

Archer's book, *Play-Making: A Manual of Craftsmanship*. In ancient times they were more developed by Euripides than by his predecessors, but that is all we need say.

Prologue; Set Speech; Messenger; there still remain two stumbling-blocks to a modern reader of Greek tragedies, the *Deus ex Mâchinâ* (or "God from the Machine") and the Chorus.

About the appearance of the god we need say little. We have seen above that an epiphany of some Divine Being or a Resurrection of some dead Hero seems to have been an integral part of the old ritual and thus has its natural place in tragedy. His special duty is to bring the action to a quiet close and to ordain the ritual on which the tragedy is based —thus making the performance itself a fulfilment of the gods' command (see above p. 65). The actual history of this epiphany is curious. As far as our defective evidence allows us to draw conclusions we can make out that Aeschylus habitually used a divine epiphany, but that he generally kept it for the last play of a trilogy; that he often had a whole galaxy of gods, and that, with some exceptions, his gods walked the floor of the earth with the other actors. (The evidence for this is given in

Miss Harrison's *Themis*, pp. 347 ff.) Sophocles moving towards a more "natural" and less ritual tragedy, used the divine epiphany comparatively little. Euripides, somewhat curiously for one so hostile to the current mythology, intensified this ritual element in drama as he did all the others. And he used it more and more as he grew older. He evidently liked it for its own sake.

There is one view about the *Deus ex Máchiná* which needs a word of correction. It is widely entertained and comes chiefly from Horace's *Ars Poetica*. It takes the *Deus* as a device—and a very unskilful one—for somehow finishing a story that has got into a hopeless tangle. The poet is supposed to have piled up ingenious complications and troubles until he cannot see any way out and has to cut the knot by the intervention of something miraculous—in this case, of a machine-made god. Now devices of this sort—the sudden appearance of rich uncles, the discovery of new wills, or of infants changed at birth and the like—are more or less common weaknesses in romantic literature. Hence it was natural that Horace's view about Euripides's god should be uncritically accepted. But as a matter of fact it is a mere mistake. It never in any single case holds good—not

even in the *Orestes*. And there are some
plays, like the *Iphigenia in Tauris*, in which,
so far from the god coming to clear up a tan-
gled plot, the plot has to be diverted at the
last moment so as to provide an excuse
for the god's arrival. Euripides evidently
liked a supernatural ending, and when he
had to do without a real god—as in the
Medea and the *Hecuba*—he was apt to end
with winged chariots and prophecies. Can
we in the least understand what he gained
by it?

We must remember one or two things.
The epiphany was in the ritual. It was no
new invention in itself; the only new thing,
apparently, was an improved piece of stage
machinery enabling the god to appear more
effectively. Further, if we try to put ourselves into the minds of fifth century Greeks,
there was probably nothing absurd, nothing
even unlikely, in supposing the visible appearance of a god in such an atmosphere as
that of tragedy. The heroes and heroines of
tragedy were themselves almost divine; they
were all figures in the great heroic saga and
almost all of them—the evidence is clear—
received actual worship. If Orestes or Agamemnon is present on the stage, it is not surprising that Apollo should appear to them.

It is, I think, chiefly due to the mistake of
over-emphasizing the realism of Euripides
that recent writers—myself at one time in-
cluded—have been so much troubled over
these divine epiphanies.

I suspect, also, that we are troubled by a
difference of convention about the way in
which supernatural beings ought to speak.
We moderns like them to be abrupt, thun-
derous, wrapped in mystery. We expect the
style of ancient Hebrew or Norse poetry.
Probably a Greek would think both barbaric.
At any rate the Greek gods, both in Euripides and elsewhere, affect a specially smooth
and fluent and lucid utterance.

And apart from the artistic convention
there is a historical consideration which we
must never forget, though we are constantly
tempted to do so. A well-educated Athenian
of the fifth century before Christ was, after
all, not as securely lifted above what he called
"primæval simplicity" as a similar man in
Western Europe in the eighteenth or nine-
teenth century after. He was just beginning,
with great daring and brilliance, to grasp at
something like a philosophic or scientific
view of the world; but his hold was very
precarious and partial, and when it slipped
he fell unsuspectingly into strange abysses.

A visible god in the theatre laid probably no more strain on his credulity than, say, a prophetic dream on ours.

However, the above considerations are only pleas in mitigation of sentence. They tend to show that the *Deus ex Máchiná* was not in itself ridiculous to the contemporaries of Euripides; we must go further and try to see why he liked it. The best way is simple, with our antecedent prejudices removed, to read and re-read some of the best epiphany scenes; those, for instance, which close the *Electra*, the *Hippolytus*, the *Rhesus* or the *Andromache*. We have already seen in the *Electra* how the poet can use his gods for delivering his essential moral judgment on the story; the condemnation of revenge, the pity for mankind, the opening up of a larger atmosphere in which the horror through which we have just passed falls into its due resting-place. In the *Hippolytus* the sheer beauty of the Artemis scene speaks for itself and makes a marvellous ending. Notably it attains an effect which could scarcely be reached in any other way, a strange poignant note amid the beauty, where mortal emotion breaks against the cliffs of immortal calm. After many words of tenderness Artemis finishes (1437 ff.):

Farewell! I may not watch man's fleeting breath,
Nor stain mine eyes with the effluence of death.
And sure that terror now is very near. . . .
    (*The Goddess slowly rises and floats away.*)

HIPPOLYTUS

Farewell! Farewell, most blessèd! Lift thee clear
Of soiling men. Thou wilt not grieve in heaven
For our long love. . . . Father, thou art forgiven;
It was Her will; I am not wroth with thee. . . .
I have obeyed her all my days!

Of course the epiphany does not give what
our jaded senses secretly demand, a strong
"curtain." It gives the antique peaceful
close. The concrete men and women whom
we have seen before us, striving and suffering,
dissolve into the beautiful mist of legend;
strife and passion and sharp cries sink away
into the telling of old fables; then the fables
themselves have their lines of consequence
reaching out to touch the present world and
the thing that we are doing now; to make it
the fulfilment of an ancient command or
prophecy, to give it a meaning that we had
never realized; and thus we are awakened to
the concrete theatre and the audience and
the life about us not with a shock but gradually, like one lying with his eyes half shut and
thinking about a dream that has just gone.

I do not for a moment say that the divine
epiphany is the right, or even the best, way

of ending any tragedy; I only plead that if
we use our imaginations we can find in it a
very rare beauty and can understand why
one of the greatest of the world's dramatists
held to it so firmly.

CHAPTER IX

AND lastly there is the Chorus, at once the strangest and the most beautiful of all these ancient and remote conventions. If we can understand the Chorus we have got to the very heart of Greek tragedy.

The objections to the Chorus are plain to any infant. These dozen homogeneous persons, old men or young women, eternally present and almost never doing anything, intruded on action that often demands the utmost privacy: their absurdity, on any plane of realism, is manifest. We need waste no more words upon it. Verisimilitude is simply thrown to the winds. That is, no doubt, a great sacrifice, and fine artists do not as a rule incur a sacrifice without making sure of some compensating gain. Let us try to find out what that gain was, or at least what the great Greek artists were aiming at. And let us

begin by forgetting the modern stage altogether and thinking ourselves back to the
very origins of drama.

The word "chorus" means "dance" or
"dancing-ground." There were such dancing
floors on Greek soil before ever the Greeks
came there. They have been found in pre-
historic Crete and in the islands. We hear in
Homer of the "houses and dancing-grounds"
of the Morning Star. The dance was as old
as mankind; only it was a kind of dance that
we have almost forgotten. The ancient dance
was not, like our ballets, rooted in sexual
emotion. It was religious: it was a form of
prayer. It consisted in the use of the whole
body, every limb and every muscle, to express
somehow that overflow of emotion for which
a man has no words. And primitive man
had less command of words than we
have. When the men were away on the war-
path, the women prayed for them with all
their bodies. They danced for the men's safe
return. When the tribe's land was parching
for lack of rain the tribesmen danced for the
rain to come. The dance did not necessarily imply movement. It might consist in
simply maintaining the same rigid attitude,
as when Moses held out his arms during the
battle with the Amalekites or Ahure in the

Egyptian story waited kneeling and fasting for Nefrekepta's return.

Now if we consider what kind of emotion will specially call for this form of expression it is easy to see that it will be the sort that tends quickly to get beyond words: religious emotions of all kinds, helpless desire, ineffectual regret and all feelings about the past. When we think of the kind of ritual from which tragedy emerged, the lament for a dead god, we can see how well a dance was fitted, in primitive times, to express the emotions that we call tragic.

This dance gradually grew into drama; how it did so is an old story. Into the inarticulate mass of emotion and dumb show which is the Dance there comes some more articulate element. There comes some one who relates, or definitely enacts, the actual death or "pathos" of the hero, while the Chorus goes on as before expressing emotion about it. This emotion, it is easy to see, may be quite different from that felt by the Hero. There is implied in the contemplation of any great deed this ultimate emotion, which is not as a rule felt by the actual doers of it, and is not, at its highest power, to be expressed by the ordinary language of dialogue. The dramatist may make his characters express all that they can properly feel; he may put into articulate dialogue all that it will bear. But there still remains some residue which no one on the stage can personally feel and which can only express itself as music or yearning of the body. This residue finds its one instrument in the Chorus.

Imagine the death of some modern hero, of Lincoln or of Nelson, treated in the Greek form. We should have first a Messenger bringing news of the battle of Trafalgar or the pistol-shot in the Washington Theatre. The hero would be borne in dying; his friends would weep over him; we should hear his last words. But there would always remain some essential emotion or reflection—sadness, triumph, pathos, thoughts of the future from which this man will be lacking or of the meaning of this death in human history: neither Lincoln nor Nelson can express this, nor without falsity any of their human companions. In a novel the author can express it; in a modern play or a severely realistic novel it is generally not expressed except by a significant silence or some symbol. For realistic work demands extreme quickness in its audience, and can only make its effect on imaginations already trained by romance and idealism. On the Greek stage the Chorus

will be there just for this purpose, to express
in music and movement this ultimate emotion and, as Mr. Haigh puts it, to "shed a lyrical splendour over the whole." It will translate the particular act into something universal. It will make a change in all that it
touches, increasing the elements of beauty
and significance and leaving out or reducing
the element of crude pain. This is nothing
extraordinary: it is the normal business of
poetry, at least of great tragic poetry. An
actual bereavement is an experience consist-
ing of almost nothing but crude pain; when
it is translated into religion or poetry, into
"Rachel weeping for her children," or into
"Break, break, break," it has somehow become a thing of beauty and even of comfort.

The important thing to observe is what
Mr. F. M. Cornford has explained in his
Thucydides Mythistoricus (pp. 144 ff.), that a
Greek tragedy normally proceeds in two
planes or two worlds. When the actors are
on the stage we are following the deeds and
fates of so many particular individuals, lovers, plotters, enemies, or whatever they are,
at a particular point of time and space.
When the stage is empty and the Choral Odes
begin, we have no longer the particular acts
and places and persons but something uni-

versal and eternal. The body, as it were, is gone and the essence remains. We have the greatness of love, the vanity of revenge, the law of eternal retribution, or perhaps the eternal doubt whether in any sense the world is governed by righteousness.

Thus the talk about improbability with which we started falls into its proper insignificance. The Chorus in Euripides is frequently blamed by modern scholars on the ground that "it does not further the action," that its presence is "improbable," or its odes "irrelevant." The answer is that none of these things constitute the business of the Chorus; its business is something considerably higher and more important.

Of action and relevancy we will speak later. They are both closely connected with the question of verisimilitude. And as for verisimilitude, we simply do not think of it. We are not imitating the outside of life. We are expressing its soul, not depicting its body. And if we did attempt verisimilitude we should find that in a Chorus it is simply unattainable. In Nelson's case a Chorus of Sailors would be every bit as improbable as a Chorus of Mermaids or Angels, and on the whole rather more strikingly so. If we try to think of the most effective Choruses in modern

tragedies, I do not think we shall hit on any
bands of Strolling Players or Flower Girls or
Church Choirs or other Choruses that aim at
"naturalness"; we shall probably go straight
to the Choruses of Spirits in *Prometheus Un-
bound* or those of The Ages and The Pities in
Mr. Hardy's *Dynasts*. The Chorus belongs
not to the plane of ordinary experience,
where people are real and act and make
apposite remarks, but to that higher world
where in Mr. Cornford's words "metaphor,
as we call it, is the very stuff of life."

With very few exceptions, Greek Choruses
are composed of beings who are naturally the
denizens or near neighbours of such a world.
Sometimes they are frankly supernatural, as
in the *Eumenides*, or half supernatural,
as in the *Bacchae;* sometimes they are human
beings seen through the mist of a great emotion, like the weeping Rachels of the *Suppliant Women;* the captives of the *Trojan Women* or the *Iphigenia;* the old men who
dream dreams in the *Heracles*. Even if they
start as common men or women, sooner or
later they become transformed.

The problem of the Chorus to Euripides
was not how to make it as little objectionable
as possible; it was how to get the greatest and
highest value out of it. And that resolves

itself largely into the problem of handling
these two planes of action, using now the
lower and now the upper, now keeping them
separate, now mingling them, and at times
letting one forcibly invade the other. I cannot here go into details of the various effects
obtained from the Chorus by Euripides; but
I will take a few typical ones, selecting in
each case scenes that have been loudly condemned by critics.

The first and most normal effect is to use
the Chorus for "relief"; to bring in, as it
were, the ideal world to heal the wounds
of the real. It is not, of course, "comic
relief," as indulged in so freely by the Elizabethans. It is a transition from horror or pain
to mere beauty or music, with hardly any
change of tension. I mean, that if the pain
has brought tears to your eyes, the beauty
will be such as to keep them there, while of
course changing their character. It is this
use of lyrics that enables the Greek playwright to treat freely scenes of horror and
yet never lose the prevailing atmosphere of
high beauty. Look at the Salamis Chorus
in the *Trojan Women* immediately following
the child's death; the lyrics between Oedipus
and the Chorus when he has just entered with
his bleeding eyes; or, in particular, the song

sung by the Chorus in *Hippolytus* just after
Phaedra has rushed off to kill herself. We
have had a scene of high tension and almost
intolerable pain, and the Chorus, left alone,
make certainly no relevant remarks.   I can
think of no relevant remark that would not
be absurd bathos.   They simply break out
(732 ff.):

> Could I take me to some cavern for mine hiding,
>   In the hill-tops, where the sun scarce hath trod,
> Or a cloud make the home of mine abiding,
>   As a bird among the bird-droves of God. . . .

It is just the emotion that was in our own
hearts; the cry for escape to some place, however sad, that is still beautiful: to the poplar
grove by the Adriatic where his sisters weep
for Phaethon; or, at last, as the song continues and grows bolder, to some place that has
happiness as well as beauty; to that "strand
of the Daughters of the Sunset,"

> Where a sound of living waters never ceaseth
>   In God's quiet garden by the sea,
> And Earth, the ancient Life-giver, increaseth
>   Joy among the meadows, like a tree.

And the wish for escape brings an actual
escape, on some wind of beauty, as it were,
from the Chorus's own world.   This is, on

the whole, the most normal use of the Choric
odes, though occasionally they may also be
used for helping on the action. For instance,
in the ode immediately following that just
quoted the Chorus gives a sort of prophetic or
clairvoyant description of Phaedra's suicide.

But the Greek Chorus does not only sing
its great odes on an empty stage; it also
carries on, by the mouth of its Leader, a certain amount of ordinary dialogue with the
actors. Its work here is generally kept unob-
trusive, neutral and low-toned. When a
traveller wants to ask his way; when the
hero or heroine announces some resolve, or
gives some direction, the Leader is there to
make the necessary response. But only within certain carefully guarded limits. The
Leader must never become a definite full-
blooded character with strongly personal
views. He must never take really effective
or violent action. He never, I think, gives
information which we do not already possess
or expresses views which could seem paradoxical or original. He is an echo, a sort of
music in the air. This comes out clearly in
another fine scene of the *Hippolytus*, where
Phaedra is listening at the door and the
Leader of the Chorus listens with her, echo-

ing and making more vibrant Phaedra's own emotion (565–600).

At times, in these dialogue scenes, an effect is obtained by allowing the Chorus to turn for a moment into ordinary flesh and blood. In the *Iphigenía in Tauris* (1055 ff.) the safe escape of Iphigenía and Orestes depends on the secrecy of the Chorus of Greek captives. Iphigenía implores them to be silent, and, after a moment of hesitation, because of the danger, they consent. Iphigenía, with one word of radiant gratitude, forgets all about them and leaves the stage to arrange things with her brother. And the captives left alone watch a sea-bird winging its way towards Argos, whither Iphigenía is now going and they shall never go, and break into a beautiful home-sick song. Similarly in the splendid finale of Aeschylus' *Prometheus* the Daughters of the Ocean, who have been mostly on unearthly plane throughout the play, are suddenly warned to stand aside and leave Prometheus before his doom falls: in a rush of human passion they refuse to desert him and are hurled into Hell.

At other times the effect is reached by emphasizing just the other side, the unearthliness of the Chorus. In the *Heracles*, for instance, when the tyrant Lycus is about to

make some suppliants leave the protection
of an altar by burning them—a kind of atro-
city which just avoided the technical religious
offence of violating sanctuary—the Chorus
of old men tries for a moment to raise its
hand against the tyrant's soldiers. It is like
the figures of a dream trying to fight—
"words and a hidden-featured thing seen in
a dream of the night," as the poet himself
says, trying to battle against flesh and blood;
a helpless visionary transient struggle which
is beautiful for a moment but would be grotesque if it lasted. Again, in the lost *Antiope*
there is a scene where the tyrant is inveigled
into a hut by murderers; he manages to dash
out and appeals to the Chorus of old men for
help. But they are not really old men; they
are only ancient echoes or voices of justice,
who speak his doom upon him, standing
moveless while the slayers come.

These examples enable us to understand a
still stronger effect of the same kind which
occurs in the *Medea* and has, until very lately,
been utterly condemned and misunderstood.
It is an effect rather reminding one of the
Greek fable of a human wrong so terrible that
it shook the very Sun out of his course. It
is like the human cry in the *Electra* (p. 155),
which shook the eternal peace of the gods in

heaven. There is something delirious about it, an impossible invasion of the higher world by the lower, a shattering of unapproachable bars.

Medea has gone to murder her children inside the house. The Chorus is left chanting its own, and our, anguish outside. "Why do they not rush in and save the children?" asked the critics. In the first place, because that is not the kind of action that a Chorus can ever perform. That needs flesh and blood. "Well," the critic continues, "if they cannot act effectively, why does Euripides put them in a position in which we instinctively clamour for effective action and they are absurd if they do not act?" The answer to that is given in the play itself. They do not rush in; there is no question of their rushing in: because the door is barred. When Jason in the next scene tries to enter the house he has to use soldiers with crowbars. The only action they can possibly perform is the sort that specially belongs to the Chorus, the action of baffled desire.

Medea is in the house; the Chorus is chanting its sublimated impersonal emotion about the love that has turned to Hate in Medea, and its dread of things to come (1267 ff.):

For fierce are the smitings back of blood once shed
  Where Love hath been: God's wrath upon them that kill,
And an anguished Earth, and the wonder of the dead
        Haunting as music still. . . .

when a sudden cry is heard within. The song
breaks short, and one woman speaks:

Hark! Did ye year! Heard ye the children's cry?
        Another.
O miserable woman! O abhorred!
        Voice of a Child within.
What shall I do? What is it? Keep me fast
From Mother!
        The Other Child.
        I know nothing. Brother! Oh,
I think she means to kill us.
        One of the Chorus.
                Let me go!
I will!—Help, help! And save them at the last!
        Child.
Yes, in God's name. Help quickly or we die!
        The Other Child.
She has almost caught me now: she has a sword.

One sees the Women of the Chorus listening
for the Children's words; then they break, as
it were, from the spell of their own supermor-
tal atmosphere, and fling themselves on the
barred door. They beat in vain against the
bars and the Children's voices cry for help
from the other side.

But the inrush of violent horror is only

tolerated for a moment. Even in the next
words we are moving back to the realm of
formal poetry:

Women Beating at the Door.
Thou stone, thou thing of iron! Wilt verily
Spill with thine hand that life, the vintage stored
  Of thine own agony!
Others.
A woman slew her babes in days of yore,
One, only one, from dawn to eventide. . . .

and in a moment we are away in a beautiful
remote song about far-off children who have
been slain in legend. That death-cry is no
longer a shriek heard in the next room. It is
the echo of many cries of children from the
beginning of the world, children who are now
at peace and whose ancient pain has become
part mystery and part music. Memory—
that Memory who was mother of the Muses
—has done her work upon it.

We see here the justification of the high
formalism and convention of Greek tragedy.
It can touch without flinching any horror of
tragic life, without failing in sincerity and
without marring its normal atmosphere of
beauty. It brings things under the great
magic of something which is hard to name,
but which I have tried in these pages to indi-
cate; something that we can think of as eter-

nity or the universal or perhaps even as Memory. For Memory, used in this way, has a magical power. As Mr. Bertrand Russell has finely put it in one of his *Essays*, "The Past does not change or strive. Like Duncan in *Macbeth* 'After life's fitful fever it sleeps well.' What was eager and grasping, what was petty and transitory, has faded away. The things that were beautiful and eternal shine out like stars in the night."

This power of transfiguration belongs in varying degrees to all poetry, but it belongs in special force to Greek Tragedy; and Greek Tragedy attains it in part by all its high religious traditions and severities of form, but most fully by means of its strangest convention, the Chorus; the band of half-embodied emotions and memories, the lyric song and the dance expressing things beyond speech. It is through this power that tragedy attains its peculiar quality of encouragement and triumph. We must not forget that Aristotle, a judge whose dicta should seldom be dismissed without careful reflection, distinguishes tragedy from other forms of drama not as the form that represents human misery but as that which represents human goodness or nobleness. If his MSS. are to be trusted he even goes so far as to say that tragedy is "the representation of Eudaimonia," or the higher kind of happiness. Of course he fully recognizes the place of death and disaster in it, and he prefers the so-called "unhappy ending." The powers of evil and horror must be granted their full scope; it is only thus that we can triumph over them. Only when they have worked their uttermost will do we realize that there remains something in man's soul which is forever beyond their grasp and has power in its own right to make life beautiful. That is the great revelation, or the great illusion, of tragedy.

It is achieved, apparently, by a combination of two extremes; in matter a full facing of tragic facts, and in form a resolute transfiguration of them by poetry. The weak artist shirks the truth by a feeble idealism; the prosaic artist fails to transfigure it. Euripides seems to me to have gone further than any other writer in the attempt to combine in one unity these separate poles. In this lies, for good or evil, his unique quality as a poet. To many readers it seems that his powers failed him; his mixture of real life and supernatural atmosphere, of wakeful thought and dreaming legend, remains a discord, a mere jar of over wrought conventions and violent realism. To others it is because of this very quality that he has earned the tremendous rank accorded him by Goethe, and in a more limited sense by Aristotle, and still stands out, as he stood over two thousand years ago, "even if faulty in various ways, at any rate clearly the most tragic of poets."

BIBLIOGRAPHY — PRONUNCIATION OF GREEK NAMES — INDEX

BIBLIOGRAPHY

TEXTS.—Murray, 3 vols., 3s. 6d. each (Oxford, 1901–1913), with brief critical notes. This edition received much help from Wilamowitz and Verrall. *Wecklein-Prinz* (Leipzig, about 1895 to 1905), edited by Dr. Wecklein from Prinz's collations of MSS.; large critical apparatus and lists of emendations. Text much altered.

FRAGMENTS.—*Fragmenta Tragicorum Graecorum* by Nauck (Leipzig, second edition, 1889): this fine book still holds the field (26s.). *Supplementum Euripideum* by H. von Arnim (Bonn, 1912). (Price 2s.) Contains the recent papyrus discoveries; a convenient and learned little book, 'defaced by metrical errors.

TEXTS WITH COMMENTARY.—Paley, 3 vols., 8s. each (Cambridge, second edition, 1880). Though old-fashioned and often based on wrong information about the MSS. and other matters this is a most sound and thoughtful work. Of the numerous modern editions (especially school editions) of particular plays we may mention *Euripides' Herakles* erklärt von Ulrich von Wilamowitz-Moellendorff (first edition, Berlin, 1889); since re-edited in two volumes. This is an epoch-making book, and together with the same author's *Analecta Euripidea* (1875) has laid the foundation for modern criticism: also

247

Verrall's Medea, Sandys' Bacchae, Keene's Electra, Powell's Phoenissae. In French, Weil's *Sept Tragédies d'Euripide;* in German Bruhn's editions of the Iphigenia in Tauris and the Bacchae deserve special note.

TRANSLATIONS.—There are complete translations of the extant plays in prose by Coleridge (Bohn) and in verse by A. Way (Macmillan). A good prose translation, which should really bring out the full meaning of the Greek, is greatly needed. By Murray there are at present translations of the following plays: Hippolytus, Bacchae, Trojan Women, Electra, Medea, Iphigenia in Tauris, Rhesus. In paper 1s. each, in cloth 2s. (George Allen).

ESSAYS, ETC.—The best starting point is Haigh's *Tragic Drama of the Greeks* (Oxford, 1896), pp. 204–321; Introduction to vol. i. of Paley's Commentary (see above); Articles in the Histories of Greek Literature by Mahaffy, Jebb (both Primer and article in Encyclopædia Britannica), Jevons, Murray. In French, the article in Croiset's *History of Literature;* P. Decharme, *Euripide et l'esprit de son Théâtre* (Paris, 1893); P. Masqueray, *Euripide et ses Idées* (Paris, 1908). In German, the "Einleitung" to Wilamowitz's *Herakles,* vol. i. (Berlin, 1889); Dieterich's article on Euripides in Pauly-Wissowa's *Real Encyclopädie* is excellent, though severely compressed and ignorant of English work; articles in the Histories of Literature by Bergk (still valuable), Christ (in Ivan Müller's Handbuch), Bethe (in Gercke und Norden's Handbuch), Wilamowitz (in *Kultur der Gegenwart*); the account in Eduard Meyer's *Geschichte des Alterthums*, vol. iv., is good. Also Ed. Schwartz, *Charakterköpfe aus der Antiken Literatur* (Leipzig, 1906), second study, very good: H. Steiger, *Euripides, seine Dichtung und seine Persönlichkeit* (Leipzig, 1912). Useful, though often uncritical is W. Nestle *Euripides, der Dichter der Griechischen Aufklärung* (Stuttgart, 1901); also *Die Philosophische Quellen des Euripides* (Leipzig, 1902). The ideas of "the Enlightenment," to which reference is often made, can be well studied in Mr. Brailsford's book in this Library, *Shelley, Godwin, and Their Circle*.

Dr. A. W. Verrall's theory of Euripides is developed in *Euripides the Rationalist* (Cambridge, 1905); *Euripides' Ion* (1890); *Four Plays of Euripides* (1905); *The Bacchantes of Euripides* (1910). See also G. Norwood, *The Riddle of the Bacchae* (London, 1908).

Murray's previous writings include the chapter in his *Ancient Greek Literature* (1898); introduction to vol. ii. of *The Athenian Drama* (George Allen, 1902). (This volume is called "Euripides" and contains, besides the translations of the Hippolytus, Bacchae and Frogs, since republished separately, an Introduction and an Appendix on the lost plays of Euripides). Introductions to his translations of separate plays: see above; *Greek and English Tragedy*, an essay in English Literature and the Classics, edited by G. S. Gordon (Oxford, 1912); and the article on Euripides in Hastings' *Encyclopaedia of Ethics and Religion*. (These writings have been sometimes quoted in the present volume.)

The Lives can best be read in the edition of the *Scholia* by Ed. Schwartz (Berlin, 1887). To this must now be added the fragments of Satyrus in *Oxyrhyncus Papyri*, vol. ix. (also contained, though without Dr. Hunt's introduction, in Arnim's *Supplementum Euripideum;* see above). The ancient references to the facts of Euripides' life are admirably collected in vol. i. of Nauck's small text of *Euripides*. See also Wilamowitz's *Herakles*, pp. 1-40.

CHRONOLOGY OF THE PLAYS.—Wilamowitz-Moellendorff, *Analecta Euripidea* (Berlin, 1875). Grace Macurdy, *The Chronology of the extant Plays of Euripides* (Columbia University, 1905).

LOST PLAYS.—Fragments in Nauck; see above. No complete translation. A good many of the lost plays are treated and fragments translated in the Appendix to Murray's *Euripides, Athenian Drama*, vol. ii.; see above. The classical work on this subject is still Welcker's *Griechische Tragoedie*, a great book: 3 vols. (Leipzig, 1839–41.) Hartung's *Euripides Restitutus*, 2 vols. (Hamburg, 1844), is uncritical and somewhat prejudiced against Welcher, but has much charm.

ANTIQUITIES, ETC.—The standard book is Haigh's *Attic Theatre*, 3rd edition, by A. W. Pickard-Cambridge (Oxford, 1907). See also *Greek Tragedy* by J. T. Sheppard (Cambridge Manuals) and *Greek Drama* by Barnet in Dent's Series.

PRONUNCIATION OF GREEK NAMES

GREEK names have mostly come to the modern world through Latin and consequently are generally given in their Latin form. Thus in Latin the K-sound was denoted by C; KH by CH, AI- by AE; OU- by U; U by Y, which is really a Greek letter taken over into Latin for this express purpose. Also one or two common terminations are given in their Latin form, Homêros becoming Homerus, Apollon Apollo, and Alexandros Alexander. This difference in writing did not mean a difference in pronunciation; the Latin *Aeschylus* was pronounced (except perhaps in the termination) exactly like the Greek "*Aiskhulos*," *Thucydides* like "*Thoukudides*."

The conventional English pronunciation follows the Latin form and pronounces all vowels and diphthongs as in English, except that E is always pronounced, and never used merely to lengthen a previous vowel: e.g., "Euripides" rhymes with "insipid ease," not with "glides," "Hermione" roughly with "bryony," not with "tone." OE and AE are pronounced as one syllable, like "ee" in "free" except when marked as two syllables, as "Arsinoë: EU as in "feud." Of the consonants C is pronounced as in English, CH as K. The only difficulty then is to know where the stress comes and what vowels are long or short.

251

By Latin custom, if the last syllable but one is long, it will have the stress (as *surprising, everlásting, Achílles, Agamémnon*); if the last syllable but one is short, the stress will be on the syllable before (as *ádamant, dángerous, Aéschylus, Thucýdides*).

In the following index *!* denotes a stressed short vowel sound, as in *cáttle, imbédded, pítiful, biólogy:* ⌃ denotes a stressed long vowel as in *cáke, creéper, spíteful, Octóber, endúrable, gýroscope.*

INDEX

[Not including the Bibliography.]

"Enlightenment," 48, 94, 114. *See* Ideas
Ephêbi, 43
Epicûrus, 20
Epiphany, 63, 155 *f.*, 158–162. *See Deus ex Máchiná*
Euripides: birth, 22, 35; death, 170 *f.*; biography, 23 *f.*; portrait, 25; father, 35; mother, 26 *f.*, 35; books, 28, 100; cave at Salamis, 28, 163; ideas, 8, 99; teachers, 50–58; as playwright, 7, 10, 85; mysticism, 8, 161; attitude to Religion, 188–192; influence after death, 10 *f.*; relation to Athens, 30 *f.*, 89, 96, 117 *f.*, 124, 164 *f.*; and Comedy, 30; attitude to women, 28, 32 *f.*, 32 *f.*, 119–124; style, 13 *f.*; technique, 123, 196 *f.*; battle pieces, 101
Euripides' Ode on Alcibiades, 111; Epitaph on those slain in Sicily, 142
Aégeus, 96
Aéolus, 77
Alcéstis, 69, 70 *f.*, 86
Alcmaéon in Corinth, 171
Alcmaéon in Psophis, 70, 72 *f.*
Aléxander, 135–137
Álope, 119
Andrómache (like "from a key"), 96, 110, 161, 208, 223
Andrómeda, 140–144
Antíope (Ï in Greek), 237
Aúge, 118
Bácchae, 9, 19, 173, 179–188, 193 *f.*
Bellerophóntes, 96, 188
Children of Héracles, 92 *f.*, 96, 208
Cretans, 78
Cretan Women, 70, 76
Cýclops, 69
Danaé, 118
Daughters of Pélias, 68 *f.*, 79
Eléctra, 150–155, 193, 217 *f.*, 223, 237
Eréchtheus, 96
Hécuba, 87–88, 141, 161, 185, 229
Hélena, 140, 144–146, 161, 190
Héracles, 97–103, 189, 195, 208, 232, 236
Hippólytus, 84–86, 161, 189 *f.*, 208, 210 *f.*, 216–219, 223, 234, 235
Íon, 78, 118–124, 190, 197
Iphigenia in Aulis, 171–179, 189

Iphigenia in Tauris, 96, 140, 143–144, 161, 208, 227, 232, 236
Medéa, 32, 79–84, 87, 141, 161, 185, 190, 204, 227, 237–240
Melaníppe, 27, 118
Oréstes, 155–160, 166, 189, 193, 227
Palamédes, 135, 137 *f.*
Phoeníssae, 146–150, 161
Rhésus, 43, 59, 223
Suppliant Women, 92–96, 109, 210, 234
Télephus, 70, 73 *f.*
Théseus, 91
Trojan Women, 128–134, 136 *f.*, 191, 210, 234, 236

Forgiveness, doctrine of, 159–162
Frazer, J. G., 63
Freedom of Thought, 57, 94
French Revolution, 116

Gellius, 25
Glover, 133
Gods, 189–190; on stage, 155 *f. See Deus ex Máchiná*
Goethe, 10, 243
Graces, The, 103
Grenfell, 24

Haigh, 230
Hardy, T., 232
Harrison, J. E., 63, 220
Hecataéus, 48
Helen, 159
Hellenism, 39
Héracles, Children of, 41. *See under* Euripides
Heraclitus, 62
Herd, The, 191 *f.*, 193
Heroes, 64 *f.*
Heródotus, 20, 39–42, 52 *f.*, 103
Hésiod, 47
Hippócrates, 21
Historical Spirit, 196 *f.*
Homer, 36, 129, 227
Horace, 220
Húbris, 62, 125
Hunt, 24
Hygíainon, 165
Hypérbolus, 108 *f.*

Ibsen, 9, 32, 204
Ideas, 44 *f.*, 115
Immortality, 35
Initiations, 35